Melissa Ambrosini is the bestselling author of *Mastering Your Mean Girl*, *Open Wide,* and *Comparisonitis*, the host of the top-rated podcast *The Melissa Ambrosini Show*, and entrepreneur. Named a "self-help guru" by *Elle*, her mission is to inspire others to unlock their full potential and create the business and life of their dreams.

Nick Broadhurst is a singer, songwriter, a former member of ARIA award-winning band Sneaky Sound System, visual artist, entrepreneur, father of two, and now author. The driving force behind all his work is the pure expression of creativity through music and the written word. *Time Magic* sees him teaming up for the first time with his wife, bestselling author, Melissa Ambrosini.

TIME MAGIC

TIME
MAGIC

MELISSA AMBROSINI
& NICK BROADHURST

HarperCollins*Publishers*

HarperCollins*Publishers*

Australia • Brazil • Canada • France • Germany • Holland • India
Italy • Japan • Mexico • New Zealand • Poland • Spain • Sweden
Switzerland • United Kingdom • United States of America

HarperCollins acknowledges the Traditional Custodians
of the land upon which we live and work, and pays respect
to Elders past and present.

First published in Australia in 2023
by HarperCollins*Publishers* Australia Pty Limited
Gadigal Country
Level 13, 201 Elizabeth Street, Sydney NSW 2000
ABN 36 009 913 517
harpercollins.com.au

A catalogue record for this book is available from the National Library of Australia

ISBN 978 1 4002 4 4072 (paperback)
ISBN 978 1 4002 4 4089 (ebook)
ISBN 978 1 4002 4 4096 (audio)

Cover design by Louisa Maggio, HarperCollins Design Studio
Cover images by Yaroslav Danylchenko/stocksy.com/4670518/4670519
Typeset in Bembo Std by Kirby Jones
23 24 25 26 27 LBC 7 6 5 4 3

For Leo and Bambi

Contents

Time for a Revolution

If you'd told either of us a few years ago that we'd one day write a book about time and how to make the most of it, we would have thought you were wildly mistaken. After all, we weren't good with time, and we never, ever felt like we had enough of it.

Take Nick — he'd just walked away from a hugely successful musical career with the band Sneaky Sound System to become a luxury real estate agent. He worked hard (he even won the title of top sales agent in the country), but it came at a price: he could barely scrape together 20 minutes on the weekend to play cricket with his young son. And even when he did, he was fielding just as many calls as he was balls.

Meanwhile, Melissa lived in a permanent state of overwhelm and stress. She was an Olympic-level people-pleaser who couldn't say no to anyone, which meant her time was always eaten up by other people's priorities while her own lay gathering cobwebs in a corner.

Put simply, we were both extremely time-poor. Even worse, we both thought that living this way was normal. Just as a fish can't see the water it's swimming in, we couldn't see the truth staring us in the face: we were both poor stewards of our time. In different ways, to be sure, but the end result was the same: we both felt rushed off our feet, as if there was barely enough time for our to-do lists, let alone for our loved ones or anything fun. And the thought of having enough time to devote to our passions and big dreams? It felt laughable.

Fast forward a decade and things have changed radically. Not in an "all at once" way — that stuff only happens in the movies. But in a "one step at a time" way. We worked out how to completely **change our relationship with time**, including how much of it we have and how we spend it. This step-by-step approach might not make for the most impressive montage on the movie screen, but it's been spectacularly effective in changing our lives.

It's also excellent news for you, because over this period, we've refined our approach, figured out what works and what doesn't, and distilled it all down into a tight edit of the most potent, effective time-related tools and techniques around. Many of them are backed by cutting-edge research — the kind of stuff that lights up scientific message boards in the geekiest parts of the internet. Many of them draw on ancient traditions — teachings and wisdom handed down over the ages and proven to work for countless people, not just over decades or even centuries, but over millennia. Best of all, *they work*. The drastic results we've seen (and that we'll be digging into in this book) are testament to that fact, along with the many success stories we'll be sharing. And you, dear friend, get to piggyback off all this, which means you get to skip the "trial and error" phase and jump straight to the good stuff — so you can see results way faster than we did and with way more ease. (Talk about a win-win!)

When we say "results," what exactly do we mean?

Well, we're not being vague or airy-fairy, that's for sure. When we talk about "results," we've got an actual, concrete answer for you.

If you follow the steps in this book, you can reclaim up to 16 years of your life.

That's 834 weeks. Or 140,160 hours. Or 8,409,600 minutes. Whichever way you look at them, they'll be all yours to do exactly what you please with them. Also…

If you follow the steps in this book, you can *add years to your life*.

Maybe a handful, maybe a few decades. It sounds like science fiction, but it's not: it's actually science. And because extra time means nothing if you're not well enough to enjoy it, we'll show you how to add life to your years while adding years to your life.

Before we go any further, let's be clear on something.

This is not a time management book.

You may have picked it up thinking that it was. You might be looking to the principles of time management for help because:

+ You're permanently stretched for time, and always feel like you don't have enough of it
+ You're killing yourself trying to "do it all," yet feel like you're getting nowhere
+ You're secretly ashamed of how much time you waste — on your phone, on social media, procrastinating, watching TV, not doing the things you know would move you forward with your goals

+ You're concerned by how easily you get distracted, and how long it takes you to recover from interruptions
+ You're last on your own list of priorities, with everyone else always coming first
+ You barely have the energy to get through your day — let alone do any of the fun, adventurous stuff that "Young You" thought your life would be filled with
+ You don't know how to rest — you have to "work" at relaxing (and you feel guilty when you do it!)
+ When you do get "me time," you literally don't know what to do with it (so you reach for your phone, numb out with food, or put on yet another load of laundry)
+ You barely recognize yourself in the mirror, and can feel your body getting achy decades sooner than you expected
+ You can't shake the idea that life is passing you by, and you're missing it
+ You're craving a spacious and fulfilling life, but don't know how to create it.

If you relate to any of these feelings and symptoms, you're absolutely in the right place. But it's not "time management" you need, it's Time Magic.

Historically speaking, the practice of time management has been about getting more done. The typical approach is to shave seconds off your tasks, swap leisure and rest for extra desk time, and ruthlessly limit all activities that aren't "productive." And to what end, you might ask, is all this slicing and dicing? Usually, the end goal is to cram even more tasks into your day. Or to answer more emails. Or to have an extra hour "free" in the evening (the fact that you're too exhausted to enjoy it is conveniently overlooked).

Here's our response to all of that: is "getting more done" really the right goal? What are you getting done? What does it mean to you? Does it fulfill you? And how do you feel as you're doing it?

Getting more things done — and doing them faster and more efficiently — won't give you the spacious, fulfilling life you crave. (It's still an important skill to have, though, for sure. And we're going to be sharing some epic tips, hacks, and strategies with you in this exact area that will have you saying to yourself, "How on earth have I gone my whole life without doing this?!")

But here's the thing: trying to escape the "time-poor" trap using those techniques alone misses the mark. It's like trying to build a house with nothing but a saw in your toolkit. Imagine how much more you could get done if you not only had a saw, but a hammer and a paintbrush too? Heck, what if you had a whole set of power tools at your disposal?!

So in this book, it's not just about **saving time**, it's also about **making _more_ time**, and **infusing all of it** — including those weeks, months, and years you've just alchemized out of nowhere — **with love, meaning, and joy**.

We call this approach "Time Magic." It can literally change your life. And in this revolutionary book, you'll learn the principles of this game-changing philosophy and how to apply them to your own life.

How This Book Works

The book is divided into five sections. Each builds on the previous section, so we recommend that you first read through them in order. Then you can dip back into any section at random when you need a refresher. But for now, although it's very tempting, resist the urge to skip ahead.

Here's a taste of what's in store for you.

PART ONE: THE GREAT DISAPPEARING ACT

First up, we'll be exploring the question that plagues modern humans, perhaps more than any other: **"Where (the heck) did my time go?!"**

In this part, we're going to uncover the *real* reasons why you feel like you've got no time (they may surprise you), reveal exactly where you're spending your hours right now (including the unexpected way you're flushing away two whole years of your life), and also reframe any flawed thought patterns you may have about time, so that you're setting yourself up for a life of spaciousness and fulfillment.

PART TWO: RABBITS OUT OF HATS

In this section, we'll skill you up with powerful, concrete strategies to answer the question: **"How can I reclaim my time?"**

Just like a magician pulling a rabbit out of a hat, we're going to surprise you by showing you the unexpected ways you can make years of your life suddenly "reappear."

To start with, you'll learn the scheduling secrets that will turn you into a champion planner, you'll meet the simplest, most effective productivity system on the planet (that's guaranteed to not only decrease your time spent at work, but also radically reduce your mental load), we'll dive deep into the world of digital hygiene to rewrite your relationship with technology (don't worry, you don't have to give up your phone for good — we'll do it on your terms), and you'll learn how to reclaim hours, months, and years of your life that were previously being frittered away.

This is where most time management books start — and stop. But we're only just beginning.

PART THREE: TIME MAGIC AND YOU

Now that you're managing your time with laser precision, the magic can really start. With extra time on your hands, the question now becomes: **"How can I make the most of it?"**

In this section of the book, we'll walk you through the process of optimizing all the important parts of your life — including your health, wealth, and work — so that you're primed for action, operating at your peak, and ready to squeeze every drop of juice out of the time you've got.

We'll be sharing so many genius hacks and tips here — stuff that we've spent years and invested hundreds of thousands to learn, including an ancient technique that will slow down your experience of time and make life feel more spacious, a simple activity you can do daily that skyrockets your creativity by 81 percent, and why it's so crucial to "know your numbers."

We'll also be sharing the greatest Time Magic Trick of all that ensures you get to spend 13 years of your life doing what you love. (Yep, 13 whole years!)

PART FOUR: REAPING THE REWARDS

You've now saved time, you've optimized every part of your life, and you're well on your way to creating the spacious, fulfilling life you've always dreamed of. The next question to answer is: **"What should I *do* with all my extra time?"**

By now, you know that the point of practicing Time Magic isn't just to keep stuffing your calendar and to-do list with more responsibilities, it's to live a life that's meaningful to you; that's stacked with joy, rest, space, relationships, connections, love, flow — whatever it is that makes life feel full and juicy to you.

So in Part Four we'll show you exactly how to do that — including how to find a hobby that you love (even if you have no idea what lights you up), why resting isn't "lazy," how to add more meaning to your life, and how to leave a legacy you're proud of.

PART FIVE: TIME ALCHEMY

This is where things go stratospheric. We're going to show you how to **alchemize** your time — as in, **how to make more of it!** That's right, we're talking about the secrets of longevity, aka how to flip the hourglass of your life, make the sand run backwards and add extra years to your life.

Science is moving so fast in this area, and there are massive gains up for grabs when it comes to extending your life span (and crucially, your health span — which we'll be diving into in depth). We've gathered scientifically backed tips and techniques which are truly the best of the best — the stuff that's been proven to turn back your biological clock. They're also things that anyone can do — even if you're brand new to this stuff and don't have a heap of spare cash.

Prepare to have your mind blown as we share the research-backed secrets of inexpensive supplements that can slow down and reverse the aging process, the specific mobility exercises scientists say can help you live to 100 and beyond, why getting uncomfortably hot and cold is an untapped pathway to epic vitality, and why the secret to adding decades to your life might just lie in the palm of your hand.

Our Promise to You is Simple

We promise to deliver more value in this book than in any other you'll read in your lifetime. (At the very least, in this decade.)

To that end:

+ We're going to show you how making small changes now can compound into huge time rewards later (so the return on investment — ROI — of reading this book is off the charts!).

+ We're only sharing strategies and techniques that are proven — either because we've tested them ourselves (and have got huge results), or because the science behind them is robust and vigorous.

+ And we're only sharing the stuff that's doable and accessible to real people in their real lives. (Because sure, we'd all love to be able to run off to a desert island and focus on nothing but our mindset or our longevity, but how many of us can actually do that?!)

Most importantly of all, we're going to show you **exactly** how to do all the steps in this book, and how they all **connect and interact**. You may have been burned in the past when a book promised the world then gave you nothing but a list of unconnected tips and lofty admonitions to "Stop scrolling your life away!" or "Follow your passion!" without ever explaining how to actually do it or how those things fit in with your existing commitments. So while you're jacked up on inspiration as you're reading, the feeling disappears when you finish the book and realize that you still don't know how to actually *achieve* the success that was dangled in front of you.

This book is the opposite of that. You'll see exactly how one technique influences another; how taking care of one area of your life (say, your digital hygiene) can lead to gains in another area (getting through your work faster and having more time off), and can then lead to yet another cool spillover benefit (like having the time to take up a hobby you find meaningful, or spending more quality time with your loved ones). We'll also show you how to become the type of person who can actually do all those things — who has the energy, health, headspace, and motivation to do it, even when life is challenging.

Put another way: it's a complete life system — and that's why it can completely change your life.

The Experts Weigh In

As podcast hosts with tens of millions of downloads, we've been in the privileged position of being able to sit across the table (or screen!) from some of the top performers in the world including athletes, *New York Times* bestselling authors, entrepreneurs, CEOs, Hollywood actors, scientists, philanthropists, doctors, and experts in health, nutrition, exercise, relationships, and more. We've been able to pick their brains, dissect what makes them tick, and unravel the skills, techniques, and mindsets that set them apart and make them the crème de la crème of their chosen fields.

After hundreds of interviews, one thing we realized is that no matter what industry they're in, these people all have something in common: they're all tremendously skilled at saving, optimizing, and expanding their time. (It's part of the secret sauce that made them such high achievers in the first place!)

So to add extra horsepower to the already high-voltage strategies within these pages, you'll find nuggets of wisdom directly from these high-fliers interspersed throughout this book — like this epic tip from Ryan Holiday:

If you want to dive even deeper and hear more from these experts, you can check out our podcasts, *The Melissa Ambrosini Show* and *The Nick Broadhurst Show* (find them wherever you listen to podcasts).

Why Did We Write This Book? Why Now? Why Us?!

Timing is everything. And the timing could not be more perfect for this book. With the COVID-19 pandemic triggering a mass reevaluation of how we spend our lives, more people than ever before are craving an answer to the age-old question: **"How do I live a meaningful life?"**

Even before the pandemic, we saw people in our team, our online community, our friendship group, and our extended families who were working their butts off but not getting the kinds of results they wanted and not living the life they dreamed of. They were drowning under the very real pressure to "do it all" and consumed by another important question: **"Why don't I have enough time for the stuff that matters to me?"**

This book came about because of those questions and those people, and it came about because of *you*. We believe it's in the best interests of everyone — the entire planet — if as many people as possible are living a life that allows them the time to do what they love, to be with their loved ones, and to devote time to their health, spirituality, relaxation, creativity, and to doing "work" that lights up their soul.

Imagine what society would look like if everyone's default mood was peaceful and happy rather than frazzled, anxious, and overwhelmed. Imagine how much less violence, abuse, addiction, relationship breakdown, debt, mindless consumption, and lifestyle-related diseases there'd be if people weren't so rushed and stressed all the time. Imagine how much more fulfilled we'd all be if rest, following our passions, and spending time with our loved ones weren't just secondary considerations to be squeezed into whatever scraps of time we have left, but were the primary foundations around which we built and scheduled our lives.

That's the kind of planet we want to live on. That's the kind of legacy we want to create for our children and our children's children.

And this book is our gift in service of that mission.

As for why you'd listen to us about this stuff? Well, we are simply two people who've consciously and deliberately created a life that we love and that's aligned with our values.

Nick's days of being a time-poor real estate agent are long gone. These days, he's a globally successful recording artist, entrepreneur, investor, and wellness nut — among many other things! As a musician, he's received acclaim from critics around the world (you may have been one of the 30 million-plus people who've streamed his music, either recorded under his own name or that of his collaborative project, ENOBE). He's also the host of the popular podcast *The Nick Broadhurst Show*. And even with all this on his plate, he still has ample room to do things like direct music videos, rock climbing, working out, biohacking, and writing a fiction novel.

Melissa, no longer people-pleasing and living in overwhelm, now spends her time doing the things that light her up — like recording episodes of her top-rated podcast, *The Melissa Ambrosini Show*; writing books (including bestsellers like *Mastering Your Mean Girl*); delivering TEDx talks; and creating life-changing products for her online community. She's banished the word "busy" from her vocabulary, she no longer puts other people's priorities before her own, and she knows exactly how to create space in her life for the stuff that matters most — like nourishing her body, spending time in nature, and being the most patient, present, and playful mama she can be.

Together, we've got two kids, daughter Bambi and son (Melissa's bonus son!) Leo. They are our world, and a huge part of the reason why we've intentionally built a life that's so spacious, so that we can enjoy them, connect with them, and feel like we're truly present for their childhood and beyond.

We also want to model for them what it looks like to live a life you love — where you spend your days doing what you're passionate about (and being rewarded handsomely for it); making a difference in other people's lives; nourishing your body, mind, and soul; taking action on your creative dreams; being with the people you care about; and still having loads of time for fun, rest, and play. So that's what we infuse all our days with ...

Which leads us to one final reason why we wrote this book: people kept asking us how the heck we did it all. Friends, family, colleagues, our communities: they'd look at us — sometimes with hope, sometimes with desperation — and ask us to share our "secrets" so that they too could start having time and space for the things they loved, and stop feeling so overloaded and overwhelmed all the time. (One friend almost moved us to tears when she said that she'd kill to have more time on her hands, but that instead, her to-do list was killing *her*.)

At first, when people asked us this question, we were puzzled. After all, we've been incorporating the principles of Time Magic into our lives for close to a decade now and this way of living is second nature to us — so we sometimes forget that not everyone knows this stuff.

But the question came up so often, we could no longer ignore it.

In that respect, this book is also our gift to our loved ones as well as to you.

We want you — we want everyone — to have the spacious, fulfilling life that you've always sensed is possible, but haven't known how to bring into reality.

We want to share these techniques with you so that you can reclaim up to **16** years of your life.

We want you to be able to share them with your children, their children, and all your loved ones.

So it's time for a revolution, we say. A Time Magic revolution. And it starts here.

PART ONE

The Great Disappearing Act

Join us for a deep dive into a question that plagues modern humans, perhaps more than any other: **"Where (the heck) did my time go?!"** Learn the real reasons why you feel like you've got no time, the surprising way you're flushing 9.2 years of your life away, why "brain FOMO" is real, the flawed thinking patterns that lead you to feel time-poor, and the simple but genius mindset shifts that will set you up for a life that feels spacious and fulfilling.

CHAPTER 1

Why Does It Feel Like I've Got No Time?!

Most people don't like to think about death much, which is perfectly understandable. But acknowledging the fact that there's an endpoint to our lives can actually be surprisingly useful. And counterintuitive as it sounds, thinking about death can help us figure out how to *live*.

So if you're willing, let's step outside our comfort zones, just for a moment, to talk about that final curtain call we'll all eventually make. We promise, the payoff for braving this somewhat bleak topic will be more than worth it. And we'll do our part to make it as pleasant and non-scary as possible. So on that note, instead of throwing around dark and serious words that might make your butt cheeks clench, let's talk about pie.

Picture a pie. Whatever kind of pie you like. (We're picturing an organic cherry pie, with a gluten-free crust, just in case you were wondering!)

Now, imagine that your pie is cut into 79 pieces.

Each of those slices represents a year of your life. That's because if you live in a developed country, the average expected life span is around 79 years.[1]

We've simplified this figure, because of course, life span is far more nuanced than one single number. (For example, if you're female, your average life span is actually 82 years, versus 75 for a male.[2] Then you can drill further down still, based on what country you live in, what year you were born, and a whole host of other factors.) But for now, let's keep it super simple and stick with the across-the-board average: the average human in the average developed country can expect to see 79 spins around the sun.

Using the science of statistics, we can break down your pie — aka your life — even further, slice by slice, to see just how much pie gets eaten up by certain activities. And the results may astonish you.

Your Life, Broken Down by Task

This chart shows how the average person in a developed country spends the majority of their life.

Activity	Time spent on activity[3]	Percent of life spent on activity
Sleeping	26 years	32.9 percent
Working	13 years, 2 months	16.7 percent
Time spent on your phone (includes social media)	12.8 years	16.2 percent
Watching TV	9.2 years	11.6 percent
Domestic duties	4.7 years	5.9 percent
Eating	3.67 years	4.6 percent
Holidays / Vacations	3.14 years	4.0 percent
School	1.6 years	2.0 percent
Romance (including lovemaking)	395 days	1.4 percent
Socializing	1 year, 3 days	1.3 percent
Commuting	1 year	1.3 percent
Exercise	180 days	0.69 percent

This is your life, broken down into hard numbers.

Keep in mind these figures are expressed in **total** time. So every reference to a "year" in the above table means *every single minute* *of that year* is taken up with that activity — 60 minutes an hour, 24 hours a day, seven days a week, for 365 days a year. (So 9.2 years watching TV equates to 80,592 hours spent staring at your flat screen!)

These numbers are only statistical averages, of course. You might spend less time on your phone but more time commuting. Or perhaps you only sleep seven hours a night, not the typical eight. We're not pretending to know the exact details of your life and circumstances, but what these stats *do* tell us is that on average, most people are spending far more time than they realize on activities that don't matter to them and that don't light up their soul.

Let's take the above table of figures and apply them to your pie …

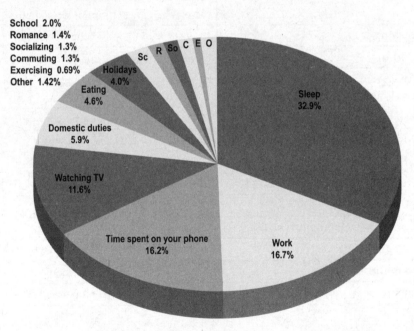

School 2.0%
Romance 1.4%
Socializing 1.3%
Commuting 1.3%
Exercising 0.69%
Other 1.42%

Sc R So C E O

Holidays 4.0%

Eating 4.6%

Domestic duties 5.9%

Watching TV 11.6%

Time spent on your phone 16.2%

Sleep 32.9%

Work 16.7%

As you can see, one-third of your pie will be devoted to sleep. Just over 16 percent is eaten up by work, and the same again on your phone.

Even though school might have felt like a significant period of your life, your actual time spent in the classroom was only 2 percent. And the average person's pie-slice devoted to exercise is so puny (0.69 percent) you have to squint to see it.

When we canvassed our community to ask what brings them the most joy in their lives, the two most common answers by a long shot were: "spending time with loved ones" and "travel." So it's sobering to see that the associated activities (vacations, romance, and socializing) only take up a combined total of 6.7 percent.

Then there are all those other things in life that you love doing (reading, playing with your kids, walks in nature, sitting in the sunshine, dancing in the kitchen, listening to music), and all the things you long to achieve (maybe learn a language, write a book, climb a mountain). When, precisely, are you meant to fit those things in?

In this tiny chunk here:

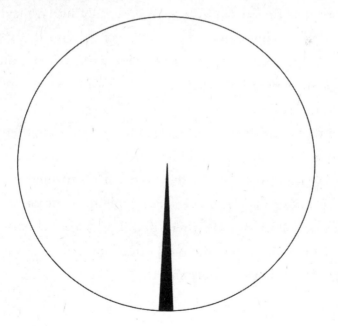

A mere 1.42 percent of your pie; 1.12 years.

That's it.

That measly little sliver is where you're meant to cram in all those things you dream about and long for, as well as any extra time you want to squeeze in with your loved ones. That's a lot to cram into just 1.42 percent of your time here on earth.

Of course, when considering these factors, it's not just your own pie that matters.

How Many Slices Has Grandma Got?

Glance sideways and have a look at the pies of the people you love. Take your parents or grandparents, for example. They're further through their pies than you. They might only have a few slices left. Which means you'll only get to celebrate a handful more Christmases with them; a handful more birthdays. You can likely count on your fingers (and if you're especially lucky, maybe your toes too) how many more times you'll get to wish them "Happy New Year" or "Shana Tova." The scary truth is that you might very well be approaching the end of your time with some of the people you love most.

Then there's the little ones in your life — your children; nieces and nephews; or any other kids close to your heart. There are only a few short years when they'll reach up to hold your hand because it makes them feel safe, or snuggle into you on the couch just because, or let you kiss them goodbye at the school gate. To paraphrase the old saying: the days might sometimes feel long, but the years can feel distressingly short!

CEO of Your Pie, Inc.

When you see all that data laid out in front of you, it can feel daunting — our time on this planet is, in the scheme of things, exceedingly short. You might even feel powerless: "My life is gonna be eaten up no matter what I do, so what's the point of even *trying* to do things differently?!"

But we want to flip that idea on its head, right here, right now. The lesson in the data table isn't that you're powerless against the pie-eating forces in your life, it's the exact opposite: **You have far more power than you may have realized, and your pie needs you to pay attention! Your pie needs you to fight for it!** Far from a lament, this is a rallying cry; a call to arms. And when it comes to the fight for your pie, you need to act like your life depends on it, because it literally does.

So before you read one page further, let's get something crystal clear: *you* are the CEO of Your Pie, Inc. — and you're a force to be reckoned with. Even though there might be parts of your life which are out of your control, and even though you may feel like there's no wiggle room to claw back any time (let alone make more of it), we hope that by the end of this book (in fact, well before that!), we'll have convinced you that, at the very least, there are so many ways you can be more *intentional* with your time, and that even small changes can have a big spillover effect that ripples through every area of your life.

Real Talk About Time

We are not here to judge, or blow smoke, or build castles on false foundations. So in case it's not clear, we want to take a moment to spell a few things out:

+ There's nothing inherently "wrong" with any of the life activities we listed above, and we're not suggesting there is. What we're focusing on are the areas where we are all flushing pie down the toilet **without realizing**. For example, if you get joy and fulfillment from spending two hours on your phone each day, that's great! (No sarcasm, we mean it.) What's *not* great is if you're spending two hours on your phone mindlessly and that amount of time concerns you. Similarly, we have our favorite TV shows that we love watching. But when we find ourselves watching too many episodes in a row or staying up past our bedtime, we know it's a signal to get extra intentional with our time.

+ None of us live in a vacuum. We exist within systems and cultures — whether we're aware of them or not — that offer unequal opportunities to some, while placing unequal burdens on others. Things like privilege and systemic racism matter, and have very real and ongoing effects that cannot be denied or ignored.

The way these systemic differences play out has a real life impact on individuals: not everyone has the same amount of control over their time, and it's overly simplistic and inaccurate to suggest that they do. This was an area we had to do some learning in a while back, but we're happy to share the lesson we learned ...

MELISSA

I'm going to get especially vulnerable with you here, so bear with me!

A while back, I shared a meme on my social media that said, "Beyoncé has the same 24 hours in the day that we do." I shared it thinking it was funny and inspirational. I thought that we all might aspire to be as kick-ass as Her Awesomeness, Beyoncé. I certainly wasn't expecting the post would spark a backlash — but it did, and I felt awful about it. So I decided to dig deeper and find out more ...

What I hadn't thought about before I shared that post is that while it's technically true, in a mathematical sense, that everyone has "the same 24 hours" on the clock each day, not everyone gets to *use* their hours in the same way. Some people's hours are consumed by things completely outside of their control — dealing with things like disability, prejudice, racism, and poverty. So for the single mother working two jobs to keep a roof over her babies' heads, and the young man in a wheelchair who takes three hours to get dressed each morning, and the Black woman dealing with hurtful microaggressions in the workplace every day for decades, is it true to say that they have "the same 24 hours" as someone like Beyoncé — who might have a housekeeper, a personal chef, a personal trainer, a chauffeur, and a myriad of other resources? From a measurement perspective, sure. In reality, no.

This was a powerful and important lesson to learn (and well worth the vulnerability hangover I'll get from sharing it!).

And the truth is, we don't even need to resort to such an extreme example as Beyoncé to find evidence of privilege when it comes to how we spend our time, the control we have over our time and the resources we bring to our time. Some people have able bodies, access to daycare for their kids, steady incomes, supportive families, trauma-free childhoods, and whatever other factors you want to consider that help us along ... and others don't have those advantages.

All of that is worth remembering.

It's important to us — and we're guessing to you too — to acknowledge the structures and systems at play in all areas of our life, including our time and how we spend it. Let's keep it in mind as we forge ahead.

Only Part of the Pie

With all the data and stats we've shared so far, we've given you a partial answer to the question of "Why the heck does it feel like I've got no time?" — because you're quite possibly spending loads of slices of your pie in ways that you weren't even aware of.

But it's not just *what* we're doing that makes us feel like we've got no time, it's also *how* we're doing those tasks, and how we think and feel about them. Yep, it's our own psychology that causes us to feel the time crunch as much as our obligations and activities. Consider the following four points.

1. TIME ANXIETY

"Time anxiety" is a colloquial term for the persistent feeling that you've never got enough time.

It can show up in a heap of different ways — perhaps you get really triggered when you run late or someone is late for you. Maybe you freak out when an unexpected curveball smashes your plans into smithereens. Or perhaps you get so overwhelmed by how little time you've got to complete your to-do list that you get paralyzed and start procrastinating. All these reactions, while multifactorial, are anchored in a belief that there's not enough time.

And here's the cruel plot twist: the more we focus on how little time we have, the scarcer our time *feels*. (And because you'll be spending time worrying, you will actually have less time for other things.) Talk about a vicious cycle!

So is the answer simply to stop focusing on how limited our time is? Unfortunately, it's not quite that simple. Deliberately trying to squash down your thoughts actually makes them more likely to surface. The technical name for this is "ironic process theory"[4] — and it's the reason why it's so crucial to shift your underlying attitudes and beliefs around time (which we'll show you how to do in the next chapter).

2. PRODUCTIVITY SHAME

Closely related to time anxiety is the phenomenon known as "productivity shame," a slang term for the intense guilt we feel when we're convinced we haven't "done enough." Nick shares his experience below.

NICK

I used to have major struggles with productivity shame.

Decades ago, when I was working as a high-end real estate agent, I fell into the trap of feeling like I was never getting enough done. I would work nine-hour days then another two to six hours most nights. I was getting loads done (probably double to triple what the average person would accomplish), and yet because I'd set such unrealistic expectations for myself, I still always felt "behind" and like I'd let myself down.

This productivity shame also meant that I felt intense guilt about doing anything I perceived as "unproductive." Taking time out to read a book or mess around on the piano felt wasteful. Doing something as "lazy" as sleeping late or bathing in the sun felt sacrilegious. And playing with my young son didn't always feel like "the best use of my time," something which I hate to admit now, but which was true back then.

In hindsight, I can see that I'd unwittingly linked my self-worth to my achievements and to how much I got done. So on that day or two each month when I actually made a big sale, I'd feel like a million bucks. And on the handful of days when I ticked a superhuman amount off my to-do list, I'd be on a high. But every other day, I'd basically spend a heap of time and energy cracking a whip over my own back in the pursuit of getting more done, at the expense of my health and my relationships.

A particularly sneaky aspect of productivity shame is that no matter how much you've achieved, *there's always more you can do*. Always. A big part of how I stepped out of the shame spiral was setting a realistic definition of how much was "enough," and learning how to feel grace and compassion for myself. So these days, if I'm feeling a bit "off" because our daughter is teething and we've all had a broken night's sleep, then I know it's okay if I only tick one or two things off my list that day — or even zero things, if my body, soul, or family need me to step away from work completely.

Another insidious element of productivity shame is that it can lead you to get bogged down in "low-value" tasks and busywork, because you get more of a thrill from ticking things off your to-do list than from making meaningful progress on a larger project that takes longer to complete. This was definitely the case for me: I'd get great satisfaction from clearing my inbox (a task which had no lasting impact on my life), yet I'd feel frustrated if I spent two hours working on a new song with no measurable outcome (even though my creative work is one of the most satisfying areas of my life, and those two hours spent "messing around" are adding to my life's work).

Does any of Nick's story sound familiar to you? If so, you're definitely not alone. And there's so much ahead in this book that will help: Chapter 2 (A Radical Reframe) will walk you through some powerful mindset shifts that will render productivity shame obsolete, Chapter 4 (Tick or Flick™) will help you do away with busywork, and Chapter 12 (Transform Your Time Off) will not only help you embrace the art of rest, but show you how vital and healthy it is to engage in activities that aren't "productive" in the traditional sense.

3. CONTINUOUS PARTIAL ATTENTION — AKA BRAIN FOMO

"Continuous partial attention" is a term coined in 1998 by tech writer Linda Stone to describe the modern predicament of being engaged in two activities at once, both of which demand brainpower — such as writing an email while listening to a podcast, or watching TV while scrolling social media.[5]

This is different from "simple multitasking" (say, eating lunch while listening to a podcast) where one of the activities is so basic and undemanding it can be performed by rote, and neither activity is impacted by the double-up.

It's also different from more complex multitasking, which actually involves repeated switching between tasks, rather than doing two things at once. (For example, when you're trying to complete two different reports for your boss at once, you might have them both open in your browser so you can jump between them at regular intervals.) We'll talk later about how inefficient this way of working is, but it's still not as cognitively draining and energetically depleting as continuous partial attention.

Continuous partial attention is like cognitive FOMO (fear of missing out). Your brain genuinely wants to be doing two things at once. It wants to engage in everything so that it doesn't miss out on anything, and in the end, you end up doing none of those things well. So even while you're hurtling down the freeway at 100 kilometers an hour with your two kids strapped in the back, you feel compelled to call your dad for a chat.

Continuous partial attention can be particularly impactful for parents — you want to pay attention to your kid, but you also want to finish that important email you've started composing. So you attempt to do both, but of course, end up doing two half-assed jobs — your child, sensing that you're not fully present, throws a tantrum, while your email is riddled with typos. (Then, of course, you're likely to start beating yourself up for being a crappy parent/worker/whatever — it's fun all round ... not!)

As Stone points out, this state of continuous partial attention creates an artificial sense of crisis — we become used to scanning our environment for the next "crucial" thing we should pay attention to, like a gazelle on the savannah who can't stop looking for lions. So our adrenaline keeps pumping, we're always in fight-or-flight mode, and everything feels like an emergency. At the same time, we never let ourselves relax, we never allow ourselves the joy and fulfillment of focusing on one thing deeply, and we never complete tasks to their full potential.

Exist in this state for long enough, and the nonstop adrenaline triggers a hormonal cascade: the stress hormone cortisol floods your system, carrying with it a host of negative spillover effects including disrupted sleep, weight gain, mood imbalance, and displacement of your happy hormones (like serotonin).[6] In short, our continuous partial attention is freaking exhausting us!

4. FULL TO THE BRIM

Thirty years ago, if you were waiting in line at the post office, the only choices available to you in those random minutes were to either chat to the person standing behind you, or to simply *wait* — to stare off into space and do nothing. These days, we all know what most people are doing in that checkout line: looking at their phones.

Like we've said, there is nothing inherently "bad" about looking at your phone. The issue we want to get at here is that we're filling up every nook and cranny of our days with *something* — frequently, with consuming media and content, where previous generations allowed themselves the glorious space of nothingness.

In fact, for so many people, the only time in their whole day where they are alone with their thoughts is in the few minutes after their head hits the pillow at night, before they fall asleep. Every other second of their day is crammed with doing, reading, consuming, and the active "filling up" of their time and their brain. (Heck, we don't even pee without our phones anymore.) Life is never going to feel spacious if we're always filling up all our spaces!

So the answer to the question "Why does it feel like I've got no time?" is multifaceted — it's both the activities that we fill our days with, and the psychology we bring to them; it's both what we're doing and how we're doing it.

So what does it all mean? How can we use this knowledge to reclaim our hours and our mental bandwidth? How can we feel as if we've got more time?

The solution is actually easy as pie: we start with our mindset. So that's exactly what we're going to do in the next chapter — we're going to rewire our thinking patterns about time.

Notes

1 www.macrotrends.net/countries/USA/united-states/life-expectancy Accessed 1st December 2022

2 www.statista.com/statistics/274507/life-expectancy-in-industrial- and-developing-countries/, Accessed 1 December 2022

3 Sources for this data: www.huffpost.com/entry/weve-broken-down-your-entire-life- into-years-spent-doing-tasks_n_61087617e4b0999d 2084fec5; www.bbc.com/news/technology-59952557; www.bls.gov/news.release/ atus.nr0.htm; www.usda.gov/media/blog/2011/11/22/how-much-time-do-americans-spend-eating; https://education.qld.gov.au/about/Documents/2023-school-calendar.pdf; mccrindle.com.au/article/blog/australians-commuting-on- average-48-minutes-per-day/; www.bostonmagazine.com/health/2016/05/03/time-spent-exercising/. (All accessed on 14 December 2022). Note that some of these averages have been further adjusted. For example, there's a sizable discrepancy between time spent on domestic duties between men and women, so we've adjusted those figures. You can find all our workings for this data on www.TimeMagic.me.

4 Wang D.A., Hagger M.S., Chatzisarantis N.L.D., "Ironic effects of thought suppression: A meta-analysis," *Perspectives on Psychological Science*, 2020;15(3):778–793. doi: 10.1177/1745691619898795

5 lindastone.net/2009/11/30/beyond-simple-multi-tasking-continuous-partial-attention/

6 lindastone.net/2009/11/30/beyond-simple-multi-tasking- continuous-partial-attention/; Cay M., Ucar C., Senol D., Cevirgen F., Ozbag D., Altay Z., Yildiz S., "Effect of increase in cortisol level due to stress in healthy young individuals on dynamic and static balance scores," *Northern Clinics of Istanbul*, 29 May 2018, 5(4):295- 301. doi: 10.14744/nci.2017.42103. PMID: 30859159; PMCID: PMC6371989

CHAPTER 2
A Radical Reframe

Consider an hour. Sixty minutes. Three thousand six hundred seconds.

What does that segment of time mean to you? Is it long or short? Is it a lot or a little?

The answer, of course, is that it depends.

If you're counting down those 60 minutes until a hot date with someone who you suspect might be the love of your life, that hour will drag on for an eternity. It's okay though, because it will be filled with anticipation, so you won't mind — it might even feel exciting!

But what about if you're running late for a meeting and get stuck in traffic? Again, every one of those 60 minutes will seem to drag on forever, but this time, it's not a pleasant experience at all. You might even find it highly stressful, your frustration rising with every passing minute.

Now imagine that you're cramming for an exam that you're massively underprepared for, but desperately need to pass. In that instance, the hour before the exam whips by at lightning speed, filling you with dread as each minute ticks by faster than you can say "C-minus."

And finally, let's say you're stuck in traffic again, but this time, you're on your way to a meeting you *really* don't want to go to. Now every minute in the peak hour gridlock seems like a reprieve; a small moment of peace before the storm. And it passes all too quickly.

In each of those situations, the exact same amount of clock time has passed: 60 minutes. Yet you experience each of those situations very differently. Time goes fast or slow, and feels enjoyable or dreadful, all because of how you perceive it and the circumstances surrounding it.

When faced with a thought experiment like this, we can all recognize, plain as day, that time is elastic. That it changes. We've all had those time-shrinking and time-expanding experiences ourselves. And yet in our day-to-day lives, it's all too easy to forget that it's our *perception* that determines our experience, and even more importantly, that we have more control over those perceptions than we may realize. Because here's the thing: your perceptions stem from your beliefs. And your beliefs about time *are* in your control. And if you don't like them — that is, if you don't like how you relate to time — it's in your power to choose a new way.

That's why we're kicking off the practical steps in this book with the three things that matter most: your thoughts, your beliefs, and your mindset. We're going to show you how to radically reframe them as they pertain to time.

It's a hugely important first step, because you won't be able to reclaim any years of your life until you've reclaimed the real estate between your ears.

So let's get started.

Introducing the Time Magic Mindset

Way too many people are stuck in a mindset that we call the **Time Scarcity Mindset**. This mindset is characterized by the overwhelming belief that there's never enough time and it's usually accompanied by a crap-ton of stress and overwhelm.

By contrast, we want to introduce you to a far more constructive, healthful, and enjoyable alternative: the **Time Magic Mindset**. This is a growth-oriented mindset that's characterized by a deep belief in your ability to invest your time in ways that are productive, nourishing, and meaningful. It's this mindset that will jump you out of always feeling time-poor and help you instead become one of the happiest, most productive, and most fulfilled people on the planet: the time-wealthy.

A TALE OF TWO MINDSETS

The best way to illustrate the difference between the Time Scarcity Mindset and the Time Magic Mindset is to show you them in action. The following snippets are all taken from real people in our real life (but we've changed their names and details to protect the individuals!).

See if you can figure out who has a Time Scarcity Mindset and who has a Time Magic Mindset:

Suzie is always busy. She moves through life with an air of chaos — frantic, frazzled, and running late. She's disorganized too, which doesn't help. Important phone numbers and addresses are scribbled on scraps of paper, only to get lost in the depths of her handbag. She's also unreliable when it comes to appointments and catch-ups. (In fact, the one thing you can rely on is that she'll be 20 minutes late!)

Seiko has one dream in life: to write a book. But she's so busy trying to do everything for everyone around her — including answering emails at all hours of the day, ferrying her kids around and fielding phone calls from her boss — that her dream constantly gets put on the backburner. This makes her feel sad and unfulfilled, like she's letting herself down.

Shane works a high-powered job that requires him to travel a lot. He rarely takes vacation time, even though he's entitled to it. Shane wants to work hard now so that he and his family can reap the rewards later, but it comes at a cost: he gets very little time with his young family. His wife and children often end up spending the school holidays at home or at the beach without him, and his marriage is struggling.

Sky is a chronic people-pleaser. Even when she's at full capacity, if someone asks her to do something, she struggles to say no. As a result, she often feels rundown and resentful of the fact that she doesn't have time for the two things she loves doing more than anything else: surfing and reading.

Shemar hasn't made time for his health in years. He works hard in his business, and at the end of the day, the tiny amount of energy he has left is spent helping his kids with their homework. As soon as they go to bed, he and his wife collapse on the couch with a bottle of pinot and watch their favorite shows for the next few hours. In the mornings when he wakes up tired and stiff, he sometimes looks in the mirror and doesn't recognize the person staring back at him.

Ming knows that she's not a naturally organized person, so she's set up some simple systems in her life to make sure that she doesn't forget things. She also knows that she tends to be a slow starter in the mornings, so she always builds in an extra buffer to enable her to start her day without rushing, and to give her at least ten minutes to sit in the sun with a cup of tea.

Mike loves his job and is aiming to one day be made partner at the law firm where he works. Recently, however, he turned down a promotion his boss offered him (even though it meant turning down a pay increase) because he came to the decision that the extra time the new role required would impact the time he could spend with his family.

Mei-Lin is passionate about yoga. For a long time, she's wanted to dive deeper into her practice and become a teacher. She recently arranged to cut back on a few hours of work each week to give her some time to start her teacher training. With smart budgeting, she and her wife have made some clever cutbacks to their weekly expenses to compensate for the slight drop in income.

Maya doesn't say yes to all the opportunities and requests that come her way. But when she does, she's "all in" and shows up fully. She recently said no to a request to help out at her son's school fete, because she knew that she wouldn't have the bandwidth to take on that role while also being the volunteer coach for the local soccer team.

Malik and his partner are both passionate runners. They sat down to write out a schedule so that both of them get to hit the trails regularly, despite both working full time and being highly engaged parents. Their solution was to alternate mornings with the kids — one day Malik gets the kids ready for school and drops them off while his partner goes for a lengthy run, then they swap over the next day. They know it's an unconventional approach, but it works for them.

We're sure you figured it out pretty quickly: all those people whose names start with "S" have a Time **Scarcity** Mindset, while all those whose names start with "M" have a Time **Magic** Mindset.

Which category do you relate to more? Are you in the same club as Suzie, Seiko, Shane, Sky, and Shemar? Or do your attitudes more closely reflect that of Ming, Mike, Mei-Lin, Maya, and Malik?

We're guessing that you'd love to be like the latter but in reality, you're more likely to fall into the first camp. That's not us being judgmental; we're simply following the data. And the data is unequivocal. It shows that 80 percent of people report feeling time-poor — the chronic feeling of having too many things to do and not enough time to do them.[1,2] That's four out of five people. If you identify as one of them, you're in the right place. So without further ado, let's start shifting you out of time scarcity and into the Time Magic Mindset that can literally change every moment of your life from here on out.

TIME MAGIC MINDSET STEP 1: ADOPT A "GROWTH MINDSET"
Prominent psychologist, professor, and author Carol Dweck was the first to observe and describe the revolutionary concept of the "growth mindset."

A **growth mindset** is when you believe that your talents can be developed and improved, whether that's through dedication, work, learning, practice, or help from others.

In contrast, a **fixed mindset** is when you believe that your talents are "fixed": that what you've got now is what you'll always have; that your talents are "gifts" that are innate and unchangeable.[3]

Research shows that those with a growth mindset tend to achieve more and experience more success than those with a fixed mindset, because the growth-oriented individuals are less concerned with things like looking smart and worrying what other people think, so they're free to pour their efforts into learning and improving.[4]

The classic example given for growth vs. fixed mindsets is intelligence: some people believe they can improve their intelligence; some people think that whatever smarts they were born with are what they'll have for life.

It also applies to your beliefs around time:

+ Do you believe that you can get better at mastering your time, or do you believe that you'll always struggle with it?

+ Do you believe you can create a spacious life, or do you believe that you'll always be rushed?

+ Do you believe you can learn better ways to deal with stress and overwhelm, or do you believe that "that's just who you are?"

In order to become a master of Time Magic, it's crucial that you start believing — *truly* believing — that you can improve how you manage and relate to time. Here are some practical ways to help you do that:

ACCEPT FAILURE

When you're trying out the skills and techniques in this book, you're bound to screw up sometimes. That's totally okay. In fact, it's great! Keep in mind that people with a fixed mindset shy away from failure, which means they often won't walk down the path to success at all. But people with a growth mindset welcome failure as feedback — they see it as a learning opportunity and walk away from it with a lesson (thereby rendering it not a "failure" at all).

STRETCH YOURSELF

Give yourself the opportunity to grow. Choose to take action on strategies within these pages that you're not quite sure you can pull off. (We bet you'll surprise yourself!)

GATHER EVIDENCE OF YOUR GROWTH

We're big believers in keeping track of our progress and metrics so that we can look back and see precisely how much we've grown. So try keeping track of how far you've come with respect to time. This could be as simple as once a week, reflecting on how time-poor or time-wealthy you felt that week, scoring yourself out of ten, and watching how that number changes over time. If it keeps improving, that's proof that you're growing.

TIME MAGIC MINDSET STEP 2: THINK LIKE AN INVESTOR

Wealthy people think carefully about where they invest their money. They read books, spend thousands consulting experts and weigh their choices carefully. Every dollar is invested consciously and deliberately — that's how those dollars turn into millions!

The Time Magic Mindset asks you to do the same thing with your time: to think consciously and deliberately about where you're investing your precious hours, minutes, and seconds; to invest your time with an expectation of a meaningful return on your investment (ROI) over the long term.

So how can you tell if an activity is a good investment of your time?

A simple question to ask yourself is: "How will Future Me feel after I do this activity?"

Say you're lying in bed, wondering if you should get up and exercise or stay under the covers. Future You is probably going to feel pretty damn excellent after going for a walk (even if right now, Present You would rather stay in bed). Conversely, Future You is likely going to feel lazy and lethargic after that hour scrolling your phone (even if right now, Present You thinks it's a swell idea).

So figure out what would make Future You proud, then go do it. (You'll thank yourself later!)

TIME MAGIC MASTER: CAL NEWPORT

Cal Newport is one of the best "time investors" that we know. He's brilliant at considering the long-term return on his time investments and making every single minute count.

Not only is Cal an associate professor of computer science at Georgetown University, he's also a *New York Times* bestselling author of seven books as well as a regular contributor to the *New Yorker*, the *New York Times* and *WIRED*; a frequent guest on NPR (National Public Radio); and the host of the popular *Deep Questions* podcast. Oh, and he's also a parent of three boys!

One of the secrets to his mega-productivity is a process called Time Blocking — a planning technique that helps him determine in advance how he invests his time.

It involves dividing up your day into blocks of time, then assigning each block to a specific task (or group of tasks), rather than simply working through your to-do list with no structure. For example, you might decide that from 9–11 a.m. every day you will devote a time block solely to writing your business proposal.

When we asked Cal to explain this for us, he said: "I'm a big believer in time blocking my workday. I give every minute a job in advance instead of just reacting to whatever happens to show up next in my inbox. This little act of intention has a big impact on how much useful work I'm actually able to accomplish."

He estimates that with this approach he gets as much done in a 40-hour time-blocked work-week as someone else might in an unstructured 60-hour work-week — how's that for a phenomenal ROI?!

TIME MAGIC MINDSET STEP 3: STOP CREATING TIME DEBT

Do you chronically underestimate how long things will take?

What about overestimating how much you can get done?

If you relate, don't worry: you're certainly not alone. Humans are notoriously poor at predicting how long it will take to complete tasks. In fact, this phenomenon is so common, it has a name: the **planning fallacy**, coined by famed psychologists Daniel Kahneman and Amos Tversky.[5]

It's really important to understand this mental bias that we all have, because if you repeatedly succumb to the planning fallacy, time debt is the only predictable outcome.

Repeatedly underestimating how long tasks will take means that you'll never allow yourself enough time to complete things, you'll always overcommit yourself, and you'll always stay stuck in that crappy cycle of stress and overwhelm.

In his 2011 book, *Thinking Fast and Slow*, Kahneman delved deeper into the causes of time-estimation error, and identified the two chief culprits that cause us to make these mistakes:

1. Not considering how long it's taken you to complete similar tasks in the past.
2. Not anticipating that you'll run into obstacles that will cause a delay or complications.

Luckily, there are three simple steps you can take to overcome these faulty thinking patterns:

1. USE A TIMER

Time how long it takes you to complete tasks that you do regularly. Do this a few times to give yourself an average, then use that average for your future estimates. This information can be really useful in both a work context (like determining how long it takes you to complete your monthly reports so that you can schedule the correct amount of time each month) as well as in a home context (like figuring out how long it takes you to get ready for bed at night so that you know when it's time to switch off the TV and start brushing your teeth).

2. ASK SOMEONE ELSE

Ask someone else to estimate how long the task will take you. Funnily enough, the planning fallacy only seems to come into play when we're estimating how long it will take *ourselves* to complete a task.[6] We're much better at estimating task lengths for other people. (In fact, we tend to overestimate those predictions rather than underestimate.)

3. BUILD IN A BUFFER

We all know that unexpected things come up — whether it's a traffic jam, a server down, a sick child, whatever! By factoring these occurrences in, you can create a buffer and give yourself some breathing room when stuff inevitably happens.

MELISSA

After the birth of our daughter, I noticed that when Bambi and I were leaving the house (say for a play date) things were getting rushed and I was feeling stressed.

It took me a while to realize that I was still operating on "old data." Pre-Bambi, I could get dressed and ready to leave the house in ten minutes flat. But with a child, it takes significantly longer — not only do I have to make sure she's ready, but I also have to pack a bunch more stuff to take with us (spare clothes, wipes, toys, snacks, etc.).

Turns out, I was not adequately factoring this extra time in, and was still expecting myself to be ready in pretty much the same amount of time as before. (No wonder I was feeling rushed!)

After timing myself a few times, I now know that for the two of us to comfortably get ready, it takes 25 minutes. To build in a buffer, I tack on five minutes to that prediction. So these days, we start getting ready 30 minutes before we want to leave the house, and the whole process has become much calmer and more enjoyable for both of us.

TIME MAGIC MINDSET STEP 4: TAKE ADVANTAGE OF COMPOUND INTEREST

Compound interest is when the interest accrued on a sum of money increases exponentially — rather than linearly — over a period of time.

You might remember studying this phenomenon in your high school math class, and seeing how tiny amounts of money invested regularly over time can add up to huge amounts.

We want you to use this principle when it comes to your time: where can you make tiny investments of your time that add up into huge results over the long term? For example:

+ How many people skip the last five minutes of their workout because they're tired?

+ How many students stop paying attention during the last 15 minutes of their classes?
+ How many people tell themselves "just five more minutes" when it comes to scrolling their phones, playing video games, or collapsing on the couch?

Consider how those tiny pockets of time can add up over the long haul. If you make those last five minutes of your workout count, and you're working out five days a week, that's an extra 1,300 minutes each year — imagine what that extra workout time will do for your strength, flexibility, and endurance over that period.

If you really want to take advantage of the compound interest effect, try *adding* an extra five minutes to your workout (or your songwriting session, or whatever deep-focused task you're doing). If most people are coasting for the last five minutes of their workout (i.e., if most people are half-assing 1,300 minutes of their workout time each year), but you're putting in an extra five minutes on top of that session length, over one year that's 2,600 extra minutes (or 43.33 extra hours) in your favor. Imagine the edge you'd be giving yourself — it's huge! That's the power of compound interest… put it to use for you (instead of against you) and you'll never look back.

TIME MAGIC MINDSET STEP 5: WATCH YOUR WORDS

Are you always saying that you "don't have time?"

Do you come home from work every day, grumbling to your partner that there "aren't enough hours in the day?"

Do you often have negative self-talk running through your head, like "I'm just so overwhelmed," "I'm always running late," or "I'm so disorganized"?

The words you speak — both to others and to yourself — hold a lot of hidden power. So pay attention to them. The next time you hear one of these sentences come out of your mouth, immediately replace it with a new belief that serves you better and that reflects your upgraded Time Magic Mindset. Try these alternatives:

+ "I always have time for what's important."
+ "I choose not to rush; I choose to take my time."
+ "I'm intentional about how I invest my time."
+ "I'm selective about what I say yes to."
+ "I'm learning to value my time more and more, and I'm improving every day."

State one of these new beliefs either in your head or out loud to help break the pattern. Try to really *feel* into it — how does it feel in your body to choose this upgraded belief instead? Who are you if this new belief becomes your reality instead of the old one? Which one do you want to be your default setting going forward?

TIME MAGIC MINDSET STEP 6: STOP LIVING ON AUTOPILOT

We'll let our friend Dr. Nicole LePera take the mic here to explain.

TIME MAGIC MASTER: NICOLE LEPERA, PhD

Dr. Nicole LePera — aka The Holistic Psychologist — is a clinical psychologist, author, and Instagram megastar. Her Time Magic Trick is to stop living your life on autopilot. She's got a powerful strategy to help you step out of "zombie mode" and start living your life consciously and intentionally:

"Most of us are living life in an unconscious, autopilot state.

We repeat automatic and habitual behaviors that don't serve us, and that make us feel 'stuck.' When we aren't conscious, it's like we're sleepwalking through life and things just happen to us. This is disempowering because it removes the power of choice.

"Navigating the world from this blind autopilot mode affects how we experience and use the minutes of our day. Many of us 'lose time' throughout our day. Our attention becomes distracted by thoughts and issues of the past or fears and worries about the future. Ultimately, far too many of us end up thinking and feeling like we 'don't have time' or simply can't commit to doing anything new.

"Consciousness is a state of awareness that allows us to truly experience life in the present and opens us up to all of the choices available in each moment. It is through consciousness that we find the ability to create new habits that will ultimately transform both ourselves and our world. To become truly aware of ourselves and the different habits directing our daily choices, we need to take a moment to disconnect from the autopilot running our day, every day.

"The exercise below will help you become more conscious and empowered. The key is to be consistent, practicing just a few minutes each day.

Daily Consciousness Check-in

Find one to two minutes in your day when you can practice being focused on and truly present in what you're doing. This could be while you are getting ready for your day, doing chores or sitting down to eat. It could mean stopping on your walk to look up at the clouds or taking a minute to appreciate the energy and smell of a candle burning on your counter. Make a conscious choice to witness the entirety of your experience in that moment."

TIME MAGIC MINDSET STEP 7:
TAKE TIME NOW TO MAKE MORE TIME FOREVER

This step builds on the concept of ROI, as introduced in Step 2 (Think Like an Investor).

Here's how it works: imagine taking one hour to do something now that will free up dozens, hundreds, even *thousands* of hours later on.

That's a pretty good return on your time investment, right?!

Throughout this book, we'll be sharing tips and strategies that may take some time to implement or set up, but the payoff down the road will be exponential. So carving out the space to take action now (even if you have to jiggle some things around in your schedule to find the hour that you need) will allow you to sit back later and reap the rewards ... which is pretty much the Time Magic philosophy in a nutshell!

NICK

A few years back, I learned the lesson of Step 7 in a very random way: from a grey jumper! Let me explain ...

I used to have a grey jumper which had an extra-wide neck. The wide neck was super comfy to wear, but it made the jumper slide off clothes hangers. The manufacturers were clearly aware of this problem because they'd sewn in two little loops, one inside each shoulder, that you could use to secure the jumper on a hanger and prevent it from falling off. But because it took an extra 3.5 seconds to use those little loops, I could never be bothered. It seemed like too much hassle. So the jumper always fell off the hanger and got caught in the runners of my wardrobe door.

Every single morning when I tried to open my wardrobe, the sliding door would get stuck on top of this jumper and I'd spend 30 seconds battling with it, swearing at it, and getting majorly frustrated. Every. Single. Morning.

If you do the math, you'll see that this was a *dreadful* investment of my time. I could have chosen to invest 3.5 seconds to solve the problem, but instead, I opted for the easy route in the first instance (ignoring those little loops) which made my life way harder down the track (fighting World War III with my wardrobe every day).

When I finally realized what was happening, I had to laugh at myself. How much of my life had I wasted fighting with the door, picking up the damn jumper, but never hanging it up properly? Would it not be smarter to just do it once and do it well?

These days, I know that whenever you get an opportunity to invest time now to save (or make) time in the future, you should jump on it. It might have taken me a while to learn this lesson, but it's one I'll never forget — and all because of that damn grey jumper!

TIME MAGIC MINDSET STEP 8: LOOK FOR REASONS WHY (NOT WHY NOT)

In this, the final step of the Time Magic Mindset (and this is a biggie), we want to acknowledge that there might be some suggestions in this book that may not at first glance seem like a good fit for you and your lifestyle.

That's totally fine. We know there's no such thing as one size fits all, and if something doesn't resonate for you, by all means skip it.

However, we don't want you to instantly dismiss things, to immediately say: "That won't work for me because I have four children/three poodles/two part-time jobs/some other reason why my life is different from yours!"

The Time Magic Mindset asks you to look for possibilities, not excuses. So instead of defaulting to "No" and resisting new ideas, try asking yourself questions like these:

+ How could I tweak this to make it work for me?
+ What would this need to look like in order to fit into my lifestyle?
+ What's the underlying lesson I can learn here?
+ How can I use my creativity to come up with a workaround?

We promise the payoff for staying open-minded and possibility-driven can bring you huge results — just like the other seven steps of the Time Magic Mindset.

Know what else can give you huge results?

The strategies we'll be sharing in Part Two, starting with the scheduling secrets that will give you the spacious life you've always dreamed of ...

Notes

1   Giurge L.M., Whillans A.V. and West C., "Why time poverty matters for individuals, organisations and nations," *Nature Human Behaviour*, 4, 993–1003 (2020). doi.org/10.1038/s41562-020-0920-z
2   Whillans A.V., "Time for happiness: why the pursuit of money isn't bringing you joy – and what will," *Harvard Business Review*, 24 January 2019, hbr.org/cover-story/2019/01/time-for-happiness
3   hbr.org/2016/01/what-having-a-growth-mindset-actually-means
4   *Ibid.*
5   Kahneman D., and Tversky A. (1979), "Intuitive Prediction: Biases and Corrective Procedures," *TIMS Studies in Management Science*, 12, 313–327

6   Buehler R., Griffin D. and Ross M., "Inside the planning fallacy: The causes and consequences of optimistic time predictions," In Thomas Gilovich, Dale Griffin & Daniel Kahneman (Eds.), 2002, *Heuristics and Biases: The Psychology of Intuitive Judgement*, pp. 250–270, Cambridge University Press. doi: 10.1017/ CBO9780511808098.016

Rabbits Out of Hats

When a magician brandishes a bunny out of their hat, the audience always gasps — something that was not there before has suddenly appeared in plain sight. Of course, on reflection, we all know that the rabbit was there all along … we just couldn't see it. In this section, we're going to do the same thing for your time by sharing powerful, actionable strategies that answer the question, **How can I reclaim my time?** And just like the gasping audience, you might be shocked by all the pockets of time — both large and small — we'll make "appear."

In this chapter, you'll learn the planning technique that makes your priorities *happen*, you'll meet the simplest, most effective productivity system on the planet, you'll learn the life-changing skill of focus, and we'll share a magical formula to help you get your work *done* — even when you're feeling resistance, don't feel like it, or are struggling with procrastination.

This is where most time management books start … and stop. But as far as Time Magic goes, we're only just beginning.

CHAPTER 3

Priority Planning

The Colorado River basin is one of the most important river systems in the US, with more than 40 million people across seven states relying on it for one of the most precious, life-giving resources known to humankind: water.

With so many people relying on this single body of water, there was conflict early on as each state tried to claim their share. Eventually, a formal contract, the Colorado River Compact, was drawn up. This agreement divvied up 15 million "acre-feet" of water (the US unit used to measure water at this scale) between the seven states, so that all of them had enough to live on.

The only problem? There are only 13 million acre-feet in the whole river system.

So if 15 million acre-feet have been allocated, but there are only 13 million acre-feet available, you may well be wondering: how on earth does the arrangement work?

The answer is, *it doesn't*. There is literally not enough water for everyone to take what they need.

So now, the river system is in a state of crisis. Entire sections have been sucked dry, drought has taken over, and the lush, green ecosystems that lined the lower regions have all but disappeared.

You might be wondering: why all this talk of rivers and acre feet?!

Well, far too many people allocate their time like the Colorado River Compact allocates water — allotting resources that simply don't exist. Which is clearly a recipe for disaster. Because here's the thing: if you're constantly trying to fit 27 hours of commitments into a 24-hour day, of course you're always going to feel overwhelmed and like you've "never got enough time," for the very simple reason that you don't.

Do this for long enough — continually allocating more time than you have, week after week, month after month — and you'll end up just like the Colorado River: sucked dry, a shell of your former self, and unable to sustain the kind of lush, bountiful, vibrant life you want.

Luckily, there are some simple, practical steps you can take to avoid and even reverse this situation, and we're going to walk you through them in this chapter. It all starts with a little something that we call Priority Planning.

The Power of Priority Planning

Most people don't plan their lives with their priorities in mind. They simply say yes to every request that comes their way, attempt to fit it all in, then nearly kill themselves trying to do everything. Along the way, their own needs come dead last —

and that's if they're even considered at all. So they "accidentally" find themselves on 15 different committees, taking on extra work projects, coaching their kid's Little League team, helping their second cousin move house, walking their neighbor's dog and volunteering for the local bake sale — then wonder why they can't find any time for themselves!

If we sound harsh, it's only because we want *you* to be harsh — with your priorities, with your boundaries, and with how you allocate one of the most precious, life-giving resources known to humankind: your time.

Priority Planning your time is the key to putting yourself back in charge of your life. It allows you to steer in the direction of your choosing, rather than being pulled along by the tide and swept in random directions. And the good news is, it's so damn effective, you'll wonder how you could possibly have gone for so long without it.

Meet "Priority Planning"

Priority Planning is based on the radically simple idea that **your priorities get scheduled first** — even when it means saying no to things, disappointing other people, or not doing "everything." It's one of the most freeing and powerful techniques we've ever developed, and we'd bet our last bliss ball that you're going to love it too.

But before we start planning, we need to identify what your priorities actually are. Start by grabbing a notepad and writing out your answers to the following two questions. (You can adjust these categories however you like, adding or subtracting so that you've got a list that fully reflects you and your life.)

1. **What's important to me that I'm already doing regularly:**
   a. For my physical health?
   b. For my mental health?
   c. For my spirituality?
   d. For my relationship?
   e. For my kids?
   f. For my pets?
   g. For my family?
   h. For my friendships?
   i. For my work/career?
   j. For my creative pursuits?
   k. For fun?
   l. For my greater life purpose?

This first part of the exercise is important. We want to identify the things that you're already doing so that you can *continue* to prioritize those things in your schedule. For example, maybe it's super important to you to drop your kids off at school each day, have dinner with your parents once a week, and go to the gym three times each week, and that's why you're already doing these things. If that's the case, fantastic — write 'em down!

2. **What do I never seem to have time for that I want to do regularly:**
   a. For my physical health?
   b. For my mental health?
   c. For my spirituality?
   d. For my relationship?

e. For my kids?

f. For my pets?

g. For my family?

h. For my friendships?

i. For my work/career?

j. For my creative pursuits?

k. For fun?

l. For my greater life purpose?

These are those things that you ache to do, that you see other people doing and wish you could too, or maybe even things that you feel "guilty" for not doing.

Think really deeply here, and allow yourself to be vulnerable. Here are some answers that we see come up a lot:

+ "See my parents more"

+ "Have regular date nights with my partner"

+ "Focus on my health"

+ "Attend all my kid's soccer matches"

+ "Start writing the novel I've been dreaming about"

+ "Hang out more with my friends"

+ "Learn how to play piano"

+ "Surf at least once a week"

+ "Have dinner as a family every night"

+ "Spend more time in nature".

You've now got two lists in front of you, containing all the actions and activities that are important to you. We'll get to your lists in a moment, but for now, let's digress for a quick story ...

Big Rocks Go First

Have you heard the story about the professor and the big rocks? Plenty of people have their own versions. Here's ours:

A philosophy professor stood in front of his class with an enormous glass jar. He then produced a bucket of big rocks, which he tipped into the jar until it was full to the brim. He looked up at the class and asked them if the jar was full. They all nodded yes.

Then he produced a bucket of small pebbles. He carefully tipped the small pebbles into the top of the jar. Though the jar had seemed full before, because the pebbles were small, they were able to fall around the edges of the big rocks and settle into the leftover spaces. Again, the professor asked the class if the jar was full. Again, they said yes.

Next, he whipped out a container of sand. The class laughed as he proceeded to pour the sand into the jar. The sand was even smaller than the pebbles, so again it was able to fall around the edges, fill the tiny spaces and fit easily into the jar. The professor looked questioningly at his class. "Is the jar full?" They were onto him this time, and called back loudly: "No!"

He smiled, and with a flourish, produced a jug of water. He poured the water into the jar, and, of course, it fitted.

The lesson, the professor told his class, is that you have to put your big rocks in the jar first. If he'd started with the water, or the sand, or the pebbles, none of the big rocks would have fitted. He looked around at his captivated students as he summed up: "In life, as in glass jars, you must take care of the big rocks first."

Priority Planning means identifying the "big rocks" in your life (which you've just done), and taking care of them first. The vast majority of people do not do this. They take care of the sand and the pebbles first, then have no time left over for their big rocks. Or worse, they take care of **other people's sand**, then barely have enough time for their *own* sand, let alone their pebbles or rocks.

One of the fundamental techniques that will help you create Time Magic is to take care of your big rocks first. But instead of putting them into a jar, we're going to put them into something else: your calendar.

Calendars: Your New Favorite Tool for Taking Action

If you've never been someone who's used a calendar consistently before, you might feel some resistance to giving it a go. And we get it: trying new things can feel daunting at times. But we think that having a calendar to guide your time is essential for a few reasons:

IT GETS YOUR COMMITMENTS OUT OF YOUR HEAD AND MAKES THEM CONCRETE.

This is important because commitments can get forgotten if you're relying on memory alone. They also take up valuable mental bandwidth.

IT ALLOWS YOU TO ACTIVELY PRIORITIZE WHAT'S IMPORTANT TO YOU.

We have a saying: "Show us your calendar, and we'll show you your priorities." If someone says that their fitness is super important to them, but they don't block off time in their calendar to exercise … is it really that important to them? This leads us to another saying we love: *If it's not scheduled, it's not happening.* If you decide you want to do something, it needs to go on your calendar. Otherwise you're probably not that serious about it.

IT KEEPS YOU ACCOUNTABLE TO YOURSELF.

Your calendar is a record of where you're spending your time and energy. If you keep scheduling something (like, say, a two-hour writing session to focus on the book you say you want to write), but you keep pushing it back, week after week, it's time to get honest with yourself: Maybe you don't actually want to write a book after all. Maybe now is not the season for you. Or maybe you do want to write it, and it is the right season for you, and you need to explore the deeper reason why you're not following through on your commitment to yourself.

The takeaway here is this: your calendar is not a passive document, it's a **tool for taking action and prioritizing what's important to you**. That's why we love them, and that's why we think you'll love having one too.

So let's dive into the nitty-gritty of how to set up your calendar and how to use it.

KICK-ASS CALENDAR SKILLS 101

The first question people ask us is: **"What sort of calendar should I use?"**

The answer is: whatever works best for you.

If you function better with a paper calendar, great: go for it.

For us, it's digital all the way. We truly believe our digital calendar is one of the reasons we're able to manage our time so effectively while running multiple businesses and a family. We stick with the basics and use Google Calendar.

"WHAT BELONGS IN MY CALENDAR?"

As a general rule, there are only two types of things that belong in your calendar:

1. **Big rocks that you wish to prioritize.** These are things you want to prioritize even though they might not *actually* be time-specific. For example, you might schedule time each morning to meditate, or play piano, or hang out with your kid, not because they have to be done at that exact time, but because they're your priority and you want to make sure that they *happen*.

2. **Things that must be done at a certain time.** These can include:

   a. Engagements with other people. This includes all appointments, meetings, scheduled calls, social gatherings, etc.

   b. Time-critical tasks. Got a task that must be performed at a specific time? That belongs in your calendar too. (Think: dropping the kids to school at 8 am.)

   c. Deadlines. Work project due at COB on Friday? This should be in your calendar as a visual reminder.

"WHAT *DOESN'T* BELONG IN MY CALENDAR?"

This has a simple answer: tasks and lists. These do *not* belong in your calendar.

Lots of people get confused on this issue, because they mix up task management and time management. So here's how we like to explain it:

+ A **task manager** is where you capture, manage, and track all your tasks. (In its very basic form, a task manager could be a simple to-do list or spreadsheet. We use an app, which we'll tell you about in the next chapter.)

+ A **time manager** is a calendar or schedule, where you capture time-sensitive commitments, events, and priorities.

If you're filling your calendar up with random to-do lists, it means you're using it as a task manager, which is not the job it's supposed to do and can lead to some messy outcomes. For example: what happens if you don't complete a task at a specific time — how do you keep track of it? How do you make sure it doesn't slide under the radar? How do you gauge its importance in terms of the greater project?

And with so many non–time-specific things jammed into your calendar, how do you get a feel for your day at a glance? How do you differentiate the stuff that actually needs to get done at a certain time from the stuff that can be done anytime? How do you breathe when your whole day looks packed to the max?!

Frankly, it's a recipe for overwhelm. So save yourself the stress and don't do it. We'll walk you through our system for ninja-level productivity shortly, but for now, keep this in mind: **calendars** manage time, **task managers** manage tasks.

And now, let's conduct your first ever …

Time Magic Priority Planning Session

This exercise will give you a clear picture of where your time is being spent right now. Here's how to do it:

1. Get your calendar out, whether it's a paper version or a digital one.
2. Ideally, pull up a weekly view, so you can see the whole next week laid out before you.

3. Go back to List 1, where you tracked the things that are important to you that you're already doing regularly. Enter these into your calendar. (Don't worry: you won't need to enter these into your calendar every week forever more. This exercise is just so that you can get an accurate snapshot of how your time is being spent right now.)
4. Now add into your calendar all your current weekly commitments. (Work, sport, dropping the kids at school — all those things you do week in, week out.)

Let's pause here for a moment. How is your calendar looking? Is it already so full that you're feeling overwhelmed just seeing everything in front of you? Or are you pleased to see plenty of white space?

5. Pull up List 2, where you tracked the things you want to be doing, but that you never seem to have time for. Pick three items off that list and schedule them in.
   a. If that's simple, and you've just slotted them in somewhere effortlessly, *awesome*. You've just put three big rocks in your schedule. In future weeks, we want you to schedule these things first, and slowly start adding in more of them as you feel called.
   b. If trying to fit these things into your schedule is like trying to stuff a king-size duvet into a kid-size cover, also awesome. You've just got a powerful insight into your time and how you're prioritizing it right now. This is valuable information. Stop trying to fit these things into your schedule for the moment (we don't want to stress you out even more!), pat

yourself on the back for gleaning a hugely valuable insight, and rest assured that help and powerful strategies to claim back white space are on their way (both in this chapter, and all the ones that follow).

INSPO-ACTION: POST-PRIORITY PLANNING REFLECTIONS

Grab your journal, and dig into the following questions:
1. How do you feel seeing all your commitments laid out in front of you in concrete form?
2. How do you *want* to feel when you're looking at your schedule?
3. What, if anything, needs to change?
4. If nothing changes, what's the cost?

Priority Planning Your Week

Now that you know what your time expenditure and commitments currently look like, you can start moving them towards where you want them to be. And again, you'll be using that same powerful tool to take action: your calendar.

Choose a day each week where you'll plan out the following week in advance. We like to do it on a Sunday. This weekly session is important: it's your chance to prioritize your big rocks, choose (as much as is possible) how you'll be spending your time, and steer your life in the direction you want it to go.

Basically, you do an abbreviated version of the Priority Planning session above. This time, however, only add the activities in your schedule that you need reminding of. (So you don't need to put in "every single thing," especially those things you already do regularly.)

Also, while you're doing this, consider your personality — some people like to have every second of their day scheduled, whereas others would find that claustrophobic. Play to your strengths here.

Get out your calendar and let's start:

1. **Put your big rocks in first.** Look, we're not silly. We know that if you need to be at your job from 9 a.m. till 5 p.m., then your big rocks are going to have to work around those parameters. But we still think it's important to show yourself that your priorities come first, not your boss's, or your clients', or anyone else's. It's a power move, even if it's just symbolic, and it lays important groundwork to help you make this mindset shift permanent. Repeat after us: "My priorities come first!"

2. **Now block off your time-sensitive commitments.** If you need to be at work from 9 a.m. to 5 p.m., you can block that off. If little Jimmy needs to be dropped at soccer practice at 4 p.m. on Thursday, block that off.

3. **Now add in any necessary extras.** Use your common sense here, and add as much detail as you like.

Each week, after you do this exercise, we want you to ask yourself those same four questions as before:

1. How do you feel seeing all your commitments laid out in front of you in concrete form?
2. How do you *want* to feel when you're looking at your schedule?
3. What, if anything, needs to change?
4. If nothing changes, what's the cost?

If you've spent too many weeks feeling stressed out and overwhelmed when you look at your schedule, it's time to get serious about change.

TIME MAGIC MASTER: MARIE FORLEO

You've just seen the power of planning your week in advance. But what about planning your days in advance? "Planning tomorrow today" is our friend Marie Forleo's Time Magic Trick — and holy smokes is it a good one!

Marie is an entrepreneur and *New York Times* bestselling author. We asked her to explain how she uses this strategy. Here's what she said:

"One of my favorite time saving habits for making sure I get the right things done — no matter how wacky and inconsistent my schedule is — is to plan tomorrow today. Once you learn how to do this for yourself, it should take you just 4–5 minutes to get done. But I've seen firsthand that when you turn this practice into a habit, it completely transforms your experience of time. You'll walk into each day focused and unflappable.

Here's all you need to do ... Before you wrap up your day, train yourself to take a few minutes and think through everything you have to get done tomorrow. Then, while it's all fresh in your mind, write down tomorrow's success plan, today. Notice I didn't call it a to-do list. I called it your success plan (a hot success mindset tip). Most of us have a negative association with to-do lists. They're often long, tedious, and make you feel exhausted just thinking about them. And often we make them too ambiguous, too long, and designed for failure. But a success plan? That sounds much more fun and exciting. Plus, that name assumes that you intend to help yourself succeed.

Here's how I usually do it. First, I open up my calendar and take a look at all the appointments that I have for the next day and the time that those appointments will take. A team call at 1p.m. for 30 minutes, an hour script review for *MarieTV* at 3:30 p.m., and a Peloton class at 6:30 p.m.

Then I write down all the projects and the tasks that I need to get done and give myself an estimate of how long I think each project or task will take. The first draft of a video script from 9 a.m.–10:30 a.m., review my social media schedule from 12–1 p.m., and some email clearout from 2:30 p.m.–3 p.m.

And finally, I make a new section at the bottom of my notepad with personal things that I need to handle for that day. For example, get Dad a birthday card and mail it, 30 minutes. Order more dog food, ten minutes. And book a haircut for the next month, about five minutes.

And that's it. When I do this, it clarifies exactly when I need to be at my desk and working, which tells me when I need to wake up, to have enough time to do my little morning routine, and get everything done without feeling rushed or stressed.

Nobody's perfect and not every day goes as planned, but this system gives you the best chance possible at making sure that your most important projects get done. Often, my days are very different — but the planning process is always the same. Taking just a few minutes in the afternoon helps me map out my success plan for the next day. That's me playing offense, not defense, with my life. It's a game changing move."

The Secret to Maintaining a Spacious Schedule: Saying No

What happens when you've worked so hard to create a schedule that aligns with your priorities, then *bam!* — you receive a handful of requests and invitations all in the one week: your colleague is having a birthday party, your mother wants you to come to dinner, and your client wants you to take on an extra project. What should you do?

Way too many of us are used to putting other people's needs before our own, so our instinct is to say yes to all requests that come in, even if we know we don't want to do them. But if you want to stop feeling stretched too thin all the time, this is your best opportunity to break the cycle.

Of course, saying no to requests can feel really hard at times, especially if you've spent a lifetime as an Olympic level people-pleaser. Luckily, saying no is a skill that you can practice and get better at, starting now!

WHEN SHOULD YOU SAY NO?

To help you evaluate a request or invitation, try asking yourself these questions:

+ Would saying yes to this mean saying no to one of my big rocks?
+ Will saying yes to this overwhelm me, use up too many resources, or push me towards burnout?
+ Am I likely to regret saying yes to this?
+ Would I be saying yes purely to avoid disappointing the other person?

TIME MAGIC TRICK FOR RECOVERING PEOPLE-PLEASERS

If your initial instinct is to say yes to everything, a good trick is to buy yourself some thinking time to evaluate the request carefully. Try these scripts on for size:

"Thank you for thinking of me, I'll check my calendar and get back to you."

"That sounds exciting. I can't give you an answer right now, but I'll be in touch by the end of the week."

"As a rule, I give myself a few days to think through requests like this. Can I let you know on Wednesday?"

If you then decide you want to say yes, then pop it in your calendar with a full heart. But if you decide that it's not a good fit, then it's your opportunity to stand up for your personal values by turning down the request.

Here are some ways to say an empowered "no" and to say it with grace and gratitude:

+ **Be clear and precise with your language.** Otherwise it might not be clear that you've said no at all!

+ **Expressing gratitude can make you both feel better.** If you are sincerely thankful for their request, try sharing that:

  "Thank you so much for thinking of me …"

  "It means so much that you'd ask me …"

  "Please let me know next time; hopefully I can help then …"

+ **A quick no is a good no.** Holding off on saying no to a request doesn't make it get any easier. If you know that you can't or don't want to do something, say no as soon as possible.

+ **You don't owe anyone a reason.** Sure, if your spouse asks if you want to book a vacation, a flat "no" might not be the healthiest response for your marriage! But for other requests, the old adage can be true: "No is a complete sentence."

+ **Don't leave the door open for negotiations if that's not your intention.** If you say, "No, I can't come to dinner this Friday," the other person might come back with an alternative option: "How about Saturday night?" If you *want* to open the discussion up for alternative arrangements, that's great. But if not, don't leave room to negotiate when you decline.

+ **If you wish, offer an alternative that suits you better.** If the request is something you want to do, get creative to see if you can make it work:

  "I'm not able to be there on the day for the bake sale, but I could drop off some muffins that morning."

  "I'm unable to take your project on at this time. Would you like a referral to someone else who may be better positioned to help?"

  "I'm unable to host the event at my house, but I'm happy to help source an alternative venue that would suit everyone."

Remember, it can be uncomfortable to disappoint someone else in order to not disappoint yourself. But your ability to create the spacious, priority-driven schedule (and life) of your dreams rises in direct proportion to your ability to tolerate that discomfort.

WHAT ABOUT WHEN YOU'RE NOT SURE?!

Not sure if an invitation or request is aligned with your priorities? We've got a genius way to help you figure it out. It's called the "Triple-T Test," which stands for **T**hink of **T**his **T**hursday. Here's how it works:

A request lands in your inbox in February, asking you to speak at a conference in October. It would require a two-hour car trip to the neighboring city, and an overnight stay. You're on the fence about it — it could be a good opportunity, but is it more effort than it's worth?

You immediately pull up your digital calendar and check out what you've got on in October. There's nothing written down for that week. *I suppose I've got space for it,* you think to yourself. So you dash off a note to the conference organizer confirming your attendance.

Seven and a half months pass. Now, when you look at that week in your calendar, it's full of all the normal aspects of life that you'd expect: there's a handful of work meetings, your kid has soccer practice, your old high school friend happens to be in town, you've got a date night planned with your partner, and you really need to take your dog to the vet. With "normal life" now visible on your schedule, the conference suddenly feels like *way* too much effort for not enough payoff, and now you're wishing like heck that you'd said no, but it's too late to back out.

Here's how this scenario would play out using the Triple-T Test:

The same request lands in your inbox in February for an October conference. You're not sure whether you should say yes or not.

You know that looking that far ahead in your diary can be misleading, because it will be gloriously spacious and can mislead you into thinking that you've got more time in the future than you do now.

But you're a smart cookie, so you decide to use the Triple-T Test — you **Think of This Thursday**.

So you say to yourself: *If the conference was this Thursday, in among all my current commitments, would I still say yes to it? Would I still want to make space for it?*

If you're still excited to do it this Thursday, then you can happily say yes to the request, knowing that you haven't lulled yourself into a false sense of future spaciousness.

But if the idea of trying to fit it in this Thursday, with everything else you have to do, just *really* doesn't seem worth it, then you have your answer: you need to say no. Because by the time October comes around, your life will have caught up with your calendar and you've just made the assessment that the payoff isn't worth it.

We love this test and use it regularly, along with everything else in this chapter.

On that note, how are you feeling about everything you've just learned? If you've been taking action along the way, congratulations: that means you've already taken powerful steps towards creating the lush, spacious life you've always dreamed of.

Now that you've set up the most important *time* management tool (aka your calendar), it's time to meet the most important *task* management tool. We're also going to introduce you to the simplest, most elegant, and powerful productivity system on the planet. It's all happening in the next chapter. Are you ready?

CHAPTER 4

Tick or Flick™

We want to blow everything you thought you knew about productivity right out of the water.

See, we believe that the way most people go about increasing their productivity is not serving them. Most people want to "get more done in less time." Which seems on the face of it a great idea, but there are two glaring issues with it.

For starters, doing more in less time can be a recipe for burnout. Pushing and hustling all the time — which is the only way most people know how to improve their productivity — is not sustainable. And it's definitely not fun.

Secondly, what if the tasks you're trying to do more of aren't actually moving you forward? What if you're unwittingly working hard on things that don't really make a difference? In that case, it doesn't matter how much you increase your productivity, you'll never get ahead, and you'll never be able to make the most of your time.

The approach we're going to share with you right now solves both these problems, so that you can be crazy productive in your personal and work life in a way that's sustainable (not soul sucking) and that actually moves you forward.

It's called Tick or Flick™, and when people ask us, "How do you do it all?", this is the answer. It's all about marrying efficiency with ease (an unbeatable combo), and it's the most powerful approach to productivity around.

Before we introduce you to the system, let's meet the tool that will set you free.

The Software That Will Set You Free

"How on earth did I ever live without this?!"

This will be you, a few days from now, once you've tried out a task management app for the first time.

If you've never used one before, a task management app is a digital app that allows you to capture, store, manage, sort and complete tasks. Put simply, it lets you take all those things you need to get done out of your head and into a system, so you can organize them, keep track of them and never let anything slide under the radar or clog up your mental bandwidth ever again.

There are hundreds of software options out there. Our favorite, and the one we can't live without, is called "Things." It's the one we recommend. (Things is a paid app. At the time of writing, it's only available on iOS. For Android users, our favorite option is "Todoist.") But there are plenty of others out there. Make sure the one you choose:

+ Is accessible on both your phone and your computer.
+ Allows you to sort tasks into groups. (These are called "Projects" in Things, but are also known by names such as "Folders," "Boards," etc.)

+ Allows you to sort those groups into larger categories. (These are called "Areas" in Things, but are also called "Themes," "Categories," etc.)

TIME MAGIC TOOLS

We'll be recommending plenty of powerful tools to you throughout this book — from apps to supplements and everything in between. Rest assured, we only recommend tools that we've used and loved ourselves, and we have no financial interest in anything we recommend.

Also, we're keenly aware that on this front, things can change quickly — new products are released, existing products change and technology moves forward in leaps and bounds.

To ensure you've always got our most current recommendations, head to www.TimeMagic.me for the most up-to-date list of what we're using and loving.

So now that you know the tool we're going to use, it's time to meet the simple but genius system that makes it all happen.

Drumroll please …

Tick or Flick™

By now you know: we're suckers for simplicity. So the Tick or Flick™ productivity system has just two simple steps:

1. The Daily Dump
2. Tick or Flick

That's it.

Don't be fooled by the simplicity, though. With these two steps guiding your way, you're going to be as productive as Steve Jobs on steroids and as Zen as a monk on a mountain.

Here's how to make the system work for you.

STEP 1. THE DAILY DUMP

Your brain is not a filing cabinet. Yet too many of us try to store and keep track of our tasks in our head. This is not only wildly inefficient, it's also really stressful.

The Daily Dump is a process for getting tasks out of your head and into your task management app. This simple act is incredibly liberating and frees up so much mental bandwidth, it's life-changing.

To set the system up, we'll do an initial "Big Dump," then from there, it's a simple "Daily Dump" that can take anywhere from 2–10 minutes and will ensure that your brain stays delightfully clear and tasks never get missed.

Like we've said, we think Things is streets ahead of other apps, so from now on, we'll be using the same language they use. But the principles still apply no matter what app you're using.

THE INITIAL BIG DUMP

1. Open up your task management app.
2. Go to the general task catchment area (it's called your "inbox" in Things).
3. Start entering every single task that is in your head, including:

+ One-off tasks, like "Book accommodation for trip"
+ Recurring tasks, like "Do daily back stretches from physio" or "Send monthly invoice"
+ Personal tasks, like "Send Grandpa a card for his birthday"

+ Work/business tasks, like "Research software options for new website"
+ Household tasks, like "Clean out cupboard in garage"
+ Following up tasks you've delegated to others, like "Make sure bookkeeper has logged monthly report"
+ Shopping lists and items you need to buy or get delivered, like "Order more dog food"
+ Bills that need paying, like "Pay car registration"
+ New habits you're trying to create, like "Go for half-hour walk"
+ Random things you don't want to forget, like "Try the new podcast Aunty Sue recommended"
+ Things you've been meaning to do for ages that you never seem to get around to, like "Book dentist appointment"

At this stage, don't worry about sorting any of the tasks or putting them into any kind of order. For now, the only thing we want to do is get them all out of your head.

TIME MAGIC TRICK: WRITE YOUR TASKS THE SMART WAY

As you're writing out your tasks, make sure to start each one with a verb (aka an action word).

Consider the difference between these two tasks:

- Aunty Sue's birthday present
- Post Aunty Sue's birthday present

Specifying the action will help you understand tasks at a glance (which is especially useful if you're not addressing a task straight away, but revisiting it days or weeks in the future).

This format also makes it much easier to take action on the task, because you've started it off with an action-oriented word.

… and that's your Big Dump done! Remember, there's no need to sort or order tasks for now; we just want to capture them.

You'll find it's incredibly freeing to enter them all into a single system. Instead of having some tasks listed in a spreadsheet, some in a random document, some on the back of an envelope and many, many others circling round in your head, you'll just have the one container — your task management app — where all your tasks live.

Also, you'll never have to worry about losing your list again, or losing track of a task. And you'll never have to devote precious brain space to remembering stuff that can so easily be managed outside your head. We've never looked back since we started using this technique, and we know you won't either.

NOW FOR YOUR DAILY DUMP

To do your Daily Dump, simply sit down for 2–15 minutes each day (we like to do it in the morning, after we've each finished our morning routines) and type every task you can think of into your task management app.

While your initial Big Dump might have taken a sizable chunk of time, your Daily Dump is typically much shorter, as you're only ever adding the tasks that have accumulated over the past day or so.

SEE IT IN ACTION

Here's an example of what Nick typed into his task management app during today's Daily Dump:

- Record new vocal line for song #3
- Call my parents about coming to dinner on Saturday
- Make plant-based nachos for dinner
- Add ideas to Chapter 3 of book

- Text Leo re: Formula 1 results
- Order new cable for Melissa's microphone
- Organize band for charity gig

You can see it's kind of random, it covers loads of different life areas, and it contains big and small tasks. You'll also notice that they all start with a verb.

Even though we both do our Daily Dump in the morning, if there are tasks swirling around our heads at any given moment, we don't mentally save them up for the next Daily Dump session — that would defeat the whole purpose of freeing up brain space! Instead, we enter them into the task management app on our phones straight away.

TIME MAGIC MASTER:
MICHAEL GREGER, MD

Our friend Dr. Michael Greger (physician, author, and professional speaker on public health issues) has developed a cool hack for entering tasks in his Things app.

Instead of typing things in, if he's out and about, he simply speaks new tasks out loud into his smartwatch. We'll let him explain:

"With a twist of the wrist I can say 'Remind' into my Apple Watch, followed by anything I want to clear out of my brain, and it propagates into the Things app on my phone and desktop computer. So anytime I come up with an idea for a book or video, something for my shopping list, something I want to remember to tell someone, I never have to write it down or later be plagued by the thought 'What was it I was so sure I wouldn't forget?' This allows for tangential thoughts to be rapidly shelved so I can concentrate on whatever task I have at hand."

Genius, right?!

So now you know Step 1 of this delightfully streamlined productivity system. Let's move on to the truly genius bit.

STEP 2. TICK OR FLICK™

There are entire books written on productivity, and we've read most of them. There is nothing wrong with any of these, however, we set out to create a super effective system that didn't require 300 pages to understand. The unique part, the bit that's going to blow your mind, can be explained in just three words: Tick or Flick™. The process is a cinch: each day after your Daily Dump, you're going to set aside some time to "Tick or Flick" the tasks you've just entered into your app. This is the step where we sort, sequence, date, and (sometimes) complete tasks. It shouldn't take more than 5–10 minutes, and trust us when we say it feels damn good to keep your life running as smoothly as a Swiss watch. You will become addicted to your daily Tick or Flick™ — we certainly are!

The "Tick" bit is super easy and fun. Start reading through the tasks you've just dumped in the collection area of your app. Whenever you come across a task that can be done in under two minutes, do it right at that moment, then tick it off your list and out of your life for good. *Taska la vista, baby!*

For anything that can't be done in under two minutes, you are going to "Flick" it somewhere to be properly organized, prioritized, and dated, if need be. In Things, this means flicking to a Project.

(Remember, a "Project" is how you group tasks together. Your app might call it a "folder," "category," "label," "type," etc.)

There are two main categories of projects:

1. Projects that take more than two steps to complete (for example, "Organize School Party" is a project that requires multiple steps/tasks, such as "Hire Vendors" and "Book Band").
2. Groups of one-off miscellaneous tasks that can be logically assembled together according to topic (for example, "Bills to Pay," where you'd add in all the individual tasks like "Pay Mortgage" and "Pay Energy Bill").

Another cool tip is to give your Projects a goal-oriented name — that way you know at a glance what all the individual tasks are building towards. It can also help keep you inspired. (So, for example, in reality, we'd never use "Bills to Pay" as the title of a project, because it sounds like a chore. Instead, we'd call it something like, "Magical Money Management." The sky's the limit when it comes to naming, but we say go for the most inspiring option you can think of!)

Projects can then be grouped together into overarching themes (known as "Areas" in Things). These are the umbrellas which cover broad areas of your life, like "Work," "Personal," "Health," "Finance," "Kids," etc.

INSPO-ACTION: SET UP YOUR TASK MANAGEMENT APP

Let's set up your commonly used "Projects" and the umbrella "Areas" that they fall into …

1. Think carefully about the broad categories that your tasks generally fall into. For example, work, personal, health, finance, kids, etc. Create a new Area in your app for each of these broad categories you've identified.

2. Now create one extra Area called "Momentum." Drag this Area to the top, so its first in line. Order your other Areas how you wish.

3. Take a moment to think of all the projects you've got going on right now. You might have a different project for each of your clients or products, along with a project for the book you're writing and that fitness goal you're focused on. Create a new "Project" for each one.

4. Some of your Projects will have an end date. If that's the case, add it in.

5. Some of your Projects won't have an end date because they're ongoing (for example, you might have a Project called "Financial" that you'll continue adding to each month), or because they're complex Projects that will stretch on for the foreseeable future (such as a product that you're developing that could take months or years). If that's the case, no date required.

6. Move all Projects with an end date to your "Momentum" Area. This allows you to see all your current, actionable Projects at a glance, right at the top of your app. Getting these things done is going to give you massive momentum.

7. Move all other Projects to whatever Area is appropriate and in order of priority.

8. Finally, give your Projects names that motivate and inspire you, to add extra fuel to your productivity fire. ('Cuz seriously, wouldn't you rather work on a project called "Maxing My Money Goals" rather than "Monthly Accounts"?!)

When you're Flicking tasks, many of them will belong to an existing Project you've set up, so they can be Flicked straight there. So to use Nick's Daily Dump as an example, the task "Add ideas to Chapter 3 of book" takes longer than two minutes to complete, so it would be added to an existing Project called "Writing Time Magic."

There will also be times when the task you've entered doesn't belong to a regular or existing Project, in which case, you should create a new Project and Flick the task into it.

TIME MAGIC TRICK: DON'T CONFUSE TASKS WITH PROJECTS

Some people get super overwhelmed by their to-do list because they fill it with items that should really be classified as Projects, not Tasks.

As an extreme example, if you put a "task" on your to-do list that said "Organize Wedding," you wouldn't even know where to start. Making this error can keep you paralyzed as your so-called "task" seems so huge and unclear, **because it should really be deemed a Project**.

Instead, chunk things down, so that each individual task is spelled out, then grouped together into a Project. So here, "Organize Wedding" is now correctly classified as a Project, and you can list all the more manageable tasks that will help you complete that Project. For example:

- Sit down with partner to discuss our budget
- Do online research to find potential venues in our city and choose our top five
- Call each venue to organize a tour
- Ask sister which florist she recommends
- Etc.

And here's a game-changing hint: if you ever feel paralyzed by a task, see if you can break it down even further.

For example, "Buy wife a birthday present" is perfectly fine to enter as a task. But if you still feel stuck, break it down even more:

- Research jewelry stores in local area
- Decide which store to visit
- Go to jewelry store
- Purchase bracelet
- Get wrapping paper from hallway cupboard
- Wrap present
- Make a birthday card

You'd be amazed how effective this chunking down process can be to catapult you out of stuckness and into action.

SORT AND SEQUENCE YOUR PROJECTS

The next step is to organize the tasks in each Project into an order that makes sense to you. There are a few things to consider here:

+ If your tasks have deadlines built into them, this will determine their order. (For example, if one bill needs to be paid by the tenth of the month, and the other on the twentieth, it's obvious which one needs to come first!) Add the due dates to the tasks, and your app will order them automatically.

+ Some tasks are dependent on other tasks being completed, so they naturally come first. (For example, "Research guitar teachers" needs to come before "Book first guitar lesson.")

+ Finally, there's a less obvious but perhaps even more important thing to consider when it comes to ordering and prioritizing. We call it the PS Factor — what tasks are you likely to **P**rocrastinate or **S**tress about? If you do these tasks first, all of a sudden that Project feels so much more do-able, you'll feel so much better every time you look at it, and you'll get a huge surge of momentum from having ticked that big, enormous task off your list.

As well as ordering the tasks *within* a Project, you should order the Projects themselves — any Projects with a due date should be ordered from earliest to latest, so that your more urgent Projects appear at the top.

AUTOMATE YOUR RECURRING TASKS

We all have tasks that repeat — perhaps every day, every week, every month, whatever.

Save yourself precious minutes (not to mention precious brain space) by setting up a "recurring task" for these items within your task management app. That way you'll never have to add it manually again, it will never get missed, and you'll feel next-level organized.

To do this, head into your app and look for the option within the individual task that allows you to make that task repeating, then select your chosen interval — daily, weekly, the first Monday of every month, etc.

We automate all kinds of recurring tasks — from yearly reminders about our anniversary, to weekly tasks like watering the houseplants, to daily ones like "do stretching routine."

TICK OR FLICK™: SEE IT IN ACTION

Example 1

When Nick was doing his morning Tick or Flick™, he saw a task he'd entered during his Daily Dump called "Organize band for charity gig."

He knew that this would actually require a bunch of different steps to complete, so he created a Project for it, and named it "Nail My Charity Performance." (See how he gave it a name that *connects him to the feeling* of completing that project? Much better than something boring like "Charity Gig.")

He positioned this Project in his "Music" Area, gave it a due date (so that he knew it was a Project with a start and finish), then brainstormed all the different steps he'd need to go through to complete the Project.

Once he put them in order, added dates as needed, and set up recurring tasks where necessary, his Project looked like this:

Nail My Charity Performance
- Call Mark (guitar) and Hannah (cello) to confirm availability
- Ask my assistant to change my flights to arrive a day before the performance
- Have my manager confirm musical specs for the night
- Organize live session music files
- Confirm rehearsal time and venue on the day before performance
- Confirm sound check on the day of performance
- Have manager confirm stylist to meet at my house morning of performance
- Do my daily vocal warm-up (repeat daily)
- Practice playing "Heaven Is A Heartbeat" (repeat daily)

As you can see, while there may be a few steps before Nick successfully nails his performance, there is now a clear path. What could have seemed huge and overwhelming is now neatly organized. You will notice he has set some of the tasks to repeat every day in the lead-up to the performance.

The starred task right at the top is the one that needs to be done today. The rest Nick knows need to be done in the order that follows.

KICK-ASS TICK OR FLICK™ TIPS

(Whew, try saying that three times fast!)

When it comes to the act of Ticking and Flicking, you need to find what works for you. But here are a few pointers we swear by:

DO IT DAILY

Schedule a 15-minute time slot in your calendar for your daily Tick or Flick™ session. That way, your task inbox will never build up to a point that overwhelms you. Do a monthly "audit."

Once a month, put aside some time to do a "Tick or Flick™ audit." Sounds serious but all you are doing is going through every item and making sure they are where they need to be. This is also a great time to look at your priorities and make sure your projects are organized in a way that is still in alignment with what you want to achieve. (For bonus points, add this monthly audit as a repeating task so you don't forget!)

DELEGATE LIKE A PRO

Spotted a task in your Inbox that can be delegated? Flick that bad boy to the person who's best positioned to complete it (either via email, voice message, or whatever task management system your workplace uses).

CAPTURE YOUR CREATIVE IDEAS

Had a cool idea while you're out walking? Enter it into your task management app straight away. You could create an "Ideas" Project (or similar) and Flick it there … however, we think that the Things app operates best as a pure productivity system, not as a storage system. For that reason, we prefer to store our ideas in a designated storage app like Evernote or the notes section of our phone. So during our next Tick or Flick™ session, we'll simply transfer the idea into the relevant Evernote notebook, then Tick that task-a-rooney right out of our inbox!

DO IT ONCE, DO IT NOW

Every time you encounter a task that can be set up to be recurring, do it right there and then.

BE A "BIRTHDAY BOSS"

Create separate tasks for all the people in your life who you want to wish happy birthday to, and set them to recur annually. For people whom we also want to send a birthday card or gift, we set the date on the automated task for two weeks *before* their birthday. Having an early reminder gives us time to organize a thoughtful gift and get it delivered directly to their doorstep. #winning

BATCH YOUR TASKS

You'll save so much time if you tackle a bunch of similar tasks at the one time. So give batching a try: if you've got a bunch of calls to make for a few different Projects, try doing them all in one hit. If you have a bunch of errands to run, again — be a one-hit wonder!

STACK UP YOUR "SCUT" TASKS

There will be times when you're not feeling as energetic or as "on" as you'd like. To counteract this, create a Project called

"Scut Work" and use it to house any tasks that don't take much brainpower. Then, the next time you're not really "feeling it," you can start attacking these tasks. This clever hack means you won't waste those low-energy times trying to achieve something that you're simply not in the mood for, and you won't waste your "on" energy on a bunch of boring-but-must-be-done tasks. (Alternatively, when you're not feeling "on" perhaps you can ditch work altogether and go for a walk or to the beach … both options have their upsides!)

TIME MAGIC MASTER: JJ VIRGIN

Our friend JJ Virgin is one of the most productive people we know. She's a celebrity nutrition expert and fitness hall of famer whose clients include the who's who of Hollywood. She's also a four-time *New York Times* bestselling author, entrepreneur, podcaster, speaker, and she regularly appears on TV shows like *The Today Show* and *Access Hollywood*.

When it comes to managing her daily tasks, JJ asks herself a unique question that we absolutely love, so we asked her to share it with you:

"The biggest thing I do to free up my time is to always check in on 'A.D.D.' — Can it be automated, can it be delegated, or better yet can it just be deleted? This frees me up to have more time to spend on my zone of genius and doing what I love."

Try asking yourself this same question the next time you're doing your Tick or Flick!

The Power of Time Magic Tasks (TMTs)

Even with a killer productivity system in place like this one, there's still a limit to how much you can get done each day.

To make sure you're focusing on the right things, during your daily Tick or Flick™ session, you're also going to identify your Time Magic Tasks, or TMTs.

Your TMTs are the mission-critical tasks that will lead to significant results. Often, they're also the tasks you want to put off, because they might seem a bit harder or take more time or brainpower to complete.

The secret to harnessing the power of TMTs is to designate only three tasks as TMTs every day, and focus on them first. Even if you get nothing else done, because you've chosen those three tasks strategically, and because you've prioritized them over other, less important, tasks, you'll be making meaningful headway on your goals each and every day.

INSPO-ACTION:
MAKE YOUR TMTs HAPPEN

Go ahead and create a Project in your app called "Time Magic Tasks" and put it at the top of all your projects. Using your TMTs Project is simple:

- Each day when you do your Tick Or Flick™, identify three tasks that, if you complete them, will move you further forward than any other task.
- Move those three tasks to your TMTs Project.
- Then get laser-focused (more on this soon) and smash through them, ticking them off as you go.

Remember, your TMTs must get done before anything else — before you respond to emails, open social media or do anything that is not going to move you forward. That's how you ensure that you're always making meaningful progress towards your big dreams and goals.

Then, every day when you actually *complete* your three TMTs (and with this system, you've given yourself every possible advantage to do exactly that, which for some people might be the first time they've been able to consistently keep promises to themselves, which is huge) you just try not to smile. Go on, we dare you!

Let's Recap This Game-Changing System

This system is simple and powerful by design. All you have to remember is:

1. Do a Daily Dump every morning (2–15 minutes)
   - Every task goes in your task management app (not in your head, not in other places, in the app only)
2. Do a daily Tick or Flick™ session (2–15 minutes)
   Go through the tasks in your app's inbox/collection area:
   a. Any tasks that will take under two minutes: do them straight away and tick them off.
   b. Any tasks that will take longer than two minutes, or have more than one step to complete: move them to an existing Project or create a new one.
   c. Any task that can be made recurring: set that up straight away.
   d. Once everything is either ticked or flicked, identify your three most crucial Time Magic Tasks.

e. Do those three TMTs first, before anything else, ticking them off as you go.

f. Feel like a rock star, because you are one.

Before we move on, one final thing.

You are a You-nicorn

We are all unique, and we all have unique circumstances. So how you integrate this system into your life is up to you.

Both of us like to do our Daily Dump and Tick or Flick™ first thing after our personal morning routines. But you might prefer to do them at some other time of the day; say, when your baby is napping or after the school run. That's totally cool.

Also, we do it every weekday. But if you only work part-time, or have some other scheduling quirk, maybe "every weekday" doesn't suit you. No worries.

We encourage you to make this system work for your unique circumstances and to adjust it to reflect your natural strengths and rhythms. It's a powerful jumping-off point that you can make your own, then use it to fly ...

Now let's move onto another important point: even though this system is a genuine game-changer when it comes to managing your tasks, freeing up headspace, and staying super organized, it only works when *you* do. It's not enough to have a kick-ass productivity system on its own; you have to follow through and do the work.

So what's the best way to do that? Let's find out in the next chapter.

CHAPTER 5

Focus-Pocus

Want to know the number one skill you can cultivate that will set you apart from everyone else, ensure you get significantly more done in less time, and move you towards your dreams faster than anything else? Focus.

Focus is the ability to pay attention to something and avoid getting distracted. If you've got this all-important ability, it's a true **force amplifier**: whatever you're doing, if you simply bring extra focus to it, you can amplify your results — often exponentially. (How's that for "focus-pocus?!")

The problem, of course, is that we live in a world of distractions. We're surrounded by devices, programs, environments, and algorithms that employ sophisticated tactics to get us distracted and keep us that way. There are huge corporations who profit from our distraction (*cough* every social media platform ever *cough*). In the face of all these focus foes, you'd be forgiven for wondering: is the battle to pay attention a losing one?

Luckily, the answer is a big *heck no*. You might need to get a little savvy to outsmart the forces attempting to thwart you, but laser-levels of focus are absolutely still possible.

Even better, because so many people don't prioritize this skill, if you can improve your focus by even just a smidgen, you're going to have a huge competitive advantage over your peers. This is because distraction doesn't just derail productivity and make tasks take longer to complete, it also erodes the quality of those tasks.[1] When you consider that the average knowledge worker spends a full 47 percent of their workday in a state of semi-distraction[2] (which means nearly half their working hours are spent doing slow, substandard work), there's so much scope here to give yourself a genuine edge.

In fact, we think that with a few Time Magic Tricks up your sleeve to master the skill of focus, you can get twice as much done as other people in the same amount of time. (Or you can get the same work done in half the time, then hit the beach from lunch onwards — you choose!)

Our focus philosophy has four phases.

Phase 1. Drop Your Backpack

Imagine trying to run a 100-meter race with a backpack on. It would be pretty hard to perform at your peak, right? Instead of all your energy going into a straight sprint to the finish line, you'd have a wiggling, jiggling backpack weighing you down, sending you off balance and drastically reducing your speed.

This same thing happens when most people sit down to do focused work. Instead of sprinting towards their metaphorical finish line with power and speed, they're laden down with a big satchel of mental clutter that makes it virtually impossible to focus.

Freeing yourself from that mental backpack is essential if you want to get laser-focused and perform at your peak. There are two ways to do this, and we suggest doing **both** daily.

1. YOUR DAILY DUMP

You learned this powerful process in Chapter 4. Every morning when you're doing your Daily Dump, you're getting all those pesky tasks out of your head and into a system where they can be dealt with. This alone will radically reduce your mental clutter. But to *really* clear out your brain so that it's immune to distraction, you're going to want to add in a second component.

2. MEDITATION

We're going to guide you through the ancient art of meditation in Chapter 9, where we dive deep into the science of how to build a better brain. For now, it's enough to know that meditation is one of the most powerful tools on the planet for decluttering your mind and priming it for deep focus. (And we can't wait to tell you more about it!)

Once your mind is clutter-free, it's time for the next phase.

Phase 2. Program Your Mind for Laser-Focus

Picture a wedge of lemon. *Really* picture it — a slice of bright yellow fruit with droplets of juice glistening on it. Now imagine bringing the lemon wedge to your lips and smelling that zesty scent as it hits your nostrils. Finally, you suck on it, the taste of citrus flooding your tongue and your lips pursing with the sudden sourness …

… Tell us, what's going on in your mouth right now?!

We're guessing that your salivary glands just went into overdrive imagining that wedge of lemon, the same way that they would have if you'd brought a piece of it to your lips in real life. That's the power of visualization. Just then, as your brain visualized eating the lemon, it directed your body to take action (i.e., to pump saliva into your mouth) *as though it were happening in real life*. This is huge. Essentially, visualization is like a "back door" into the engine room of your brain, allowing you to program your brain to do something in real life simply through the power of imagining it.

Athletes have long known the power of visualization (or "imagery," as it's often known in the sporting world). An extensive body of research shows that athletes who visualize a successful performance prior to competing experience a wide range of benefits including improved performance, increased frequency of training, higher levels of confidence, quicker recovery from injury, and even — you guessed it — significantly increased focus.[3]

To harness the power of imagery for yourself, try this simple but highly effective visualization before you start a focused work session.

TIME MAGIC TRICK: VISUALIZATION FOR LASER-FOCUS

1. Close your eyes, and sit somewhere comfortable with your back supported. (If you work at a desk, that's the perfect spot to do this exercise.)
2. Visualize yourself doing your work with uncompromising laser-focus. What does that look like? What does that feel like in your body?
3. One of the coolest benefits of visualization is being able to "rehearse" how you'll deal with obstacles or setbacks, so

let's do that now. Continuing with your eyes shut, picture yourself in a state of peak focus. How will you deal with interruptions? What will you do to prevent them? How will you cope with any setbacks that may occur?

4. Now visualize yourself at the end of your work session. You've maintained impressive levels of focus the entire time and have achieved what you set out to. Imagine the sense of satisfaction flooding through you. Really feel how great that sensation is inside your body.

Now that your internal environment is primed for success, it's time to set your sights on your external environment.

Phase 3. Engineer Your Environment for Focus

If you were trying to eat healthily, you wouldn't keep a stack of chocolate bars on your kitchen bench, would you? No, you'd get those items out of your kitchen (or at the very least, out of your sight). If you were smart, you'd also fill your fridge with delicious fruit and veggies to make it as easy as possible to achieve your goal.

The same principles apply when you're trying to focus: you can make your life so much easier — and the odds of reaching your goal so much higher — by engineering your environment for success. And when it comes to focus, that means eliminating all distractions from your workspace.

ELIMINATE NOISE DISTRACTIONS

Noise-canceling headphones are a great way to block out sounds that would otherwise distract you, like your kids playing, the TV blaring next door, or the doorbell ringing. If you want to take this hack to the next level, do as Nick does and be a "one hit wonder" ...

NICK

A simple yet powerful hack I use to enhance my focus is to listen to one song on repeat. Whenever I have to knuckle down and do deep work, I put on my headphones and use this hack. (Well, unless I'm working on my own music, of course!)

Most of my writing for this book has been done listening to one of my songs, "Heaven is a Heartbeat," due to its down tempo, almost "meditative" soundscape. As soon as I hear that song, I know it's laser-focus time, and my body and brain pretty much instantly slide into a heightened state of productivity.

ELIMINATE WORKSPACE DISTRACTIONS

Your workspace — which might be an office or desk, but could also be a studio, work bench, kitchen, whatever — needs to be distraction free.

Ideally, the only thing that should be in your field of vision are the tools you need for your work. For example, a laptop, a notepad, and a pen. Everything else (including papers, books, magazines, and other clutter) should be out of sight.

TIME MAGIC TRICK: FLY YOUR FOCUS FLAG

A study from the University of California found that nurses who donned bright orange vests emblazoned with the words "Do not interrupt" while they were performing complicated tasks experienced a whopping 88 percent reduction in work errors. That's huge!

If you want to try this hack out during your next focused work session, consider having an easy-to-spot "signal" that signifies to your colleagues, your kids, or whoever's around you, that you're in focus mode. You don't need to follow the nurses' lead exactly (although if you want to wear a neon orange vest, be our guest!). Instead, your "signal" could be wearing headphones, putting a sign on the door or even donning a particular hat or beanie.

In our household, if one of us is wearing our noise-canceling headphones, it would take a full-blown calamity for the other to interrupt them. That's how much value we place on cultivating and maintaining a state of focus.

ELIMINATE SCREEN DISTRACTIONS

If your focused work takes place at a computer, do not set yourself up for distraction by leaving 17 different browser windows open. Shut down every tab and window except the ones that are essential to the current task you're working on, and turn off all notifications on your computer.

ELIMINATE INBOX DISTRACTIONS

Unless you work in a role where email is a specific part of your deliverables (for example, if you are a customer service rep whose entire job is to answer customer emails as they come in), then email should not be a part of your focused work sessions. Shut it down!

ELIMINATE DIGITAL DISTRACTIONS

Your phone is a weapon of mass distraction. When it comes to staying focused, it's arguably the most destructive force you'll encounter. An easy solution? Make putting your phone out of sight a nonnegotiable part of your "getting ready to work" ritual.

As you're going through whatever steps you usually go through to prepare for a work session — booting up your computer, making a cup of tea, putting on your concentration music, and visualizing your success — make it a habit to put your phone in your desk drawer on silent. Or better yet, put it in another room entirely.

Until this habit becomes second nature, you might want to put a physical note in your workspace to prompt you — a Post-it note reminder on your desk works a treat.

Your phone — and the social media apps lurking on it — is such a significant source of distraction that we're going to devote an entire chapter to it next. But for now, if it's out of sight, you're off to a good start!

TIME MAGIC TRICK: GET A PASSWORD MANAGER

It's so frustrating when you're trying to focus on your work and get a task done but you can't open whatever app/program/account you need to access because you've forgotten your password.

Eliminate this particular focus-breaker forever (and free up valuable brains space) by getting a password manager. We use and love 1Password®. To us, it's indispensable — and well worth the money it costs each month. It lets us instantly and securely access all the digital parts of our life from any of our devices. The peace of mind is priceless!

Phase 4. Schedule Ignition Intervals

Question: What week are you likely to get the most done at work?
Answer: The week before a vacation.

Nobody wants to head away on a much-anticipated beach vacay only to be consumed with guilt over half-finished tasks. No way. The week before a vacation, we're betting you (like most people) are "all in": you're laser-focused on what you need to get done, you're immune to distractions and you display iron-willed discipline. The end result? You easily finish off your work, then feel free as a bird the following week as you wiggle your toes on that white sandy beach. *Aaaaahhhh!*

Now imagine what would happen if you brought that same level of focus and commitment to your work not *just* before a holiday, but *always* — just for a few hours per day, or even per week. How much sooner would you achieve your goals? And how much more time could you spend away from work doing things you love?!

The answers to these questions don't need to be hypothetical. You can see for yourself how enormous the difference is. The secret is to create space in your schedule for something we like to call **"Ignition Intervals."**

Have you heard of interval training? It's when you alternate intensity levels during an exercise session, so you might run as fast as you can for 30 seconds, then walk for 30 seconds, then repeat. It's a hugely effective form of training that can improve an athlete's fitness and speed faster than traditional training.

We've brought this same principle to the workplace, and the effect on our output and goals has been outrageous. Ignition Intervals are sessions scheduled in your workday where you bring that *"I'm about to go on vacation!"* energy and hyper-focus to your work.

By keeping these sessions relatively short, 1–3 hours max, you can avoid burning yourself out, get amazingly large amounts of deep work done, and make more progress on your work projects that you may have ever thought possible. (The reason we call them "Ignition Intervals" is because they ignite your goals like nothing else!)

A few tips for your Ignition Intervals:

+ Set a timer at the start of your session, and don't stop until you've hit your goal time.

+ If you do get distracted or interrupted, don't beat yourself up. Simply bring yourself back to the work at hand at the first moment of awareness.

+ Don't mistake the energy of being laser-focused and disciplined with the energy of being rushed and frantic. These work sessions are *not* about racing to get things done while your adrenal glands kick into overdrive. Instead, they are about calmly committing all your focus to the task at hand and not letting anything sway your focus.

+ After your Ignition Interval, reward yourself with a shift in gears. If possible, take a proper break — get outside, have a big drink of water, and let yourself relax.

+ Start small if you need to. Even if you just do an hour-long session or even 30 minutes, that's fine — and you'll still be outperforming most of your peers!

+ If you're an employee, consider chatting to your boss about these sessions. Let them know that where possible, you'd like to devote (for example) 9.30 a.m. to 11.30 a.m. every day to doing hyper-focused work, and you'd appreciate it if meetings could be scheduled after this time. (If your boss expresses any doubts about this arrangement, your increased work output and quality should put those to rest.)

+ Schedule your Ignition Intervals during your weekly Priority Planning session. Then guard that time as fiercely as a lion guarding its cubs. (And spoiler alert: sometimes the person you'll need to guard against most is yourself.) Treat it as sacred; as though your life depends on it — because if you want to create the life of your dreams, it does!

Ignition Intervals, like so much in this book, can change your life. Try them for yourself and prepare to be gobsmacked at how much meaningful progress you make towards your goals.

Finally, before we wrap up this chapter, we want to answer a question that we hear a lot, about a very real obstacle that stops people from achieving hyperfocus and fulfilling their full potential.

TIME MAGIC TRICK: THE FIVE-MINUTE FORMULA

"But what about those times when all I want to do is procrastinate?!"

Even with the best of intentions, even when you've scheduled an Ignition Interval and engineered your environment for maximum focus, sometimes it's inevitable that procrastination rears its ugly head and tries to jeopardize your progress.

The next time this happens, we suggest you use the Time Magic **Five-Minute Formula**. We have this formula stuck up over our shared desk. It looks like this:

$$5m \times C = F3$$

It stands for this:

5 minutes (of) Courage = Freedom, Fulfillment, and Forward Movement

When it comes to getting things done, getting *started* is usually the hardest part. But this simple equation is designed to blast through that initial difficulty so that you can overcome your internal resistance and get some momentum going.

All you have to do is summon up enough courage to sit down, take action (even a small action, it doesn't matter), and tolerate discomfort for a measly **five minutes**. That's it. Nine times out of ten, that alone is enough to blast through those cobwebs, get you in the zone, and have you raring to complete your full session.

In the rare instances where you complete your five minutes of courage and still feel unable to focus, consider choosing an easier project to work on or take a break. Whichever option you choose, you can then circle back to your Ignition Interval later in the day and try again.

But truly, trust us when we say: five minutes of courage, when done repeatedly, can change your life forever.

With all the techniques and hacks you've just learned, you've now got the tools to generate genuine "focus-pocus" and get more meaningful work done than you ever have before.

But there's one specific source of distraction we need to talk about in more depth. It's something that's eroding our focus at an alarming rate, shattering our attention spans, and swallowing up entire years of our life.

Scarily, you've probably got one of these "weapons of mass distraction" in your pocket right now.

So let's be courageous for a few more minutes and delve into a topic that so many people in the modern world struggle with: their relationship with their smartphone.

Notes

1   Draheim C., Hicks K.L., and Engle R.W., "Combining Reaction Time and Accuracy: The Relationship Between Working Memory Capacity and Task Switching as a Case Example," *Perspectives on Psychological Science*, 2016, 11(1), 133–155. doi: 10.1177/1745691615596990; Foroughi C.K., Werner N.E., Nelson E.T. and Boehm-Davis D.A. "Do interruptions affect quality of work?", *Human Factors: The Journal of the Human Factors and Ergonomics Society*, 2014, 56(7), 1262–1271. doi: 10.1177/0018720814531786

2   Killingsworth M.A., Gilbert D.T., "A wandering mind is an unhappy mind," *Science*, November 2010, 12;330(6006):932. doi: 10.1126/science.1192439. PMID: 21071660

3   Blankert T. and Hamstra M.R.W., "Imagining Success: Multiple Achievement Goals and the Effectiveness of Imagery," *Basic and Applied Social Psychology*, 2017, 39:1, 60–67, doi: 10.1080/01973533.2016.1255947

CHAPTER 6

Digital Drain

Want to hear something truly shocking? In early 2022, the BBC reported that the average person spends a third of their waking hours on their mobile phones.[1] That's 4.8 hours per day! A mind-boggling amount of time to scroll away.

There's good news, though: with so much time wastage happening, it's an area of our lives that offers huge potential for Time Magic, and where we can pull some serious rabbits out of hats.

So let's reverse the digital drain that's taking over our lives, starting with something that might feel a bit uncomfortable at first: getting face-to-face with your "numbers."

How Much Time Do You Spend on Your Smartphone, Really?

You might have read the previous statistic and immediately thought: "There's no way that *I* spend that much time on my phone!" Or maybe you thought the opposite.

Either way, there's an easy method to nail down exactly how many hours you're frittering away on your phone — iPhone users can simply check the "Screen Time" app, while Android users should check their "Digital Wellbeing" app. Select the weekly tab (iPhone users: it's down at the bottom!) and look for these two metrics:

1. Your average daily screen time
2. Your average number of daily "pick-ups"

Go check now. (We'll wait!) Now consider:

+ How many hours are you spending on your phone each day?
+ How many times are you picking up your phone?
+ Are those numbers what you expected?
+ And more importantly, how do those numbers make you feel?

We'll admit that when we first did this experiment and came face to face with our screen time numbers, we were more than a little horrified. The numbers staring us in the face were definitely higher than we expected. And when we asked our friends and family to check their numbers, they too found the results to be significantly higher than they'd anticipated. This tells us two things: firstly, that we humans are pretty shoddy at mentally tracking how we spend our time; and secondly, that our phones are one of the biggest time-sucks around!

To put the scale of that time-suck into hard figures for you, consider this. If someone gets their first phone at age 15 and spends the average amount of time on it each day (4.8 hours), that adds up to **12.8 years spent on their phone** over the course of their lifetime.[2]

Of course, 4.8 hours per day is just the average. A US study found that 13 percent of millennials and 5 percent of baby boomers report spending over 12 hours every day on their phones— that's like flushing nearly half your life down the toilet![3]

We don't know about you, but for us, our screen time numbers were unacceptable. The thought of flushing away that much time truly scared us, and we knew we needed to take some big action steps to reclaim that time and rewrite our relationship with technology as a whole.

But that's when we started to run into trouble.

Easily Said, Not So Easily Done

In case you haven't noticed, it's not that easy to simply "use your phone less."

The truth is that our phones and many of the common apps most of us use daily — in particular, social media apps — are addictive. And we're not throwing that word around lightly, we mean it literally: phones and apps are designed to be addictive. Tech companies use the same tactics that casinos use to reel you in and keep you staring at the screen, and every element of your digital experience — from the audible ping of your notifications, to those little "hearts" and "likes" on your posts, to the "infinite scroll" feature we've all come to accept as normal — is engineered to trigger a tidal wave of reward and pleasure neurotransmitters in our brains (in particular, dopamine — known as "the molecule of more") that turn us into literal junkies.

Researchers from the University of Maryland's International Centre for Media and the Public Agenda conducted a study in which college students were asked to go without their phones, tablets, and other devices for 24 hours. Even in this short time, students reported having "withdrawal symptoms" and many participants said that it felt like they were trying to "kick a hard drug habit," with one student reporting: "I was itching, like a crackhead, because I could not use my phone."[4]

If that's not scary enough for you, consider all the other problems associated with excessive smartphone usage, including impaired vision,[5] musculoskeletal disorders,[6] sleep deficit,[7] insomnia,[8] stress,[9] anxiety,[10] depression,[11] mental health disorders,[12] obesity,[13] and reduced cognitive capacity[14] — and believe us: those are just the tip of the iceberg.

So what are we to do? If our smartphones are devices of addiction, does that mean we're all doomed to be forever glued to our screens, throwing away giant chunks of our lives?

No, absolutely not. But it does mean that we have to be extra aware and get extra strategic in order to outsmart the forces that are actively trying to rob us of our time. Before we share the powerful strategies that can change the game, let's address a question that might be running through your mind ...

"ARE YOU ABOUT TO TELL ME I CAN NEVER USE MY PHONE AGAIN?!"

Absolutely not. Let's get super clear about something: the goal of this chapter is not to get you to stop using your phone entirely or to feel guilty every time you pick it up; far from it. What we want is for you to stop losing time mindlessly, without realizing it, and to start using your phone intentionally and on your terms.

So if you love to watch cat videos on your phone and it brings you joy, that's great. We'll readily admit that sometimes there's no better feeling than kicking back on the couch and scrolling through a heap of interior design posts (Melissa) or watching obscure indie music videos (Nick).

The trap we're focused on helping you avoid is that crappy feeling when you sit down, start scrolling (maybe because you're procrastinating, or because you simply can't think of anything better to do), then you look up and realize that a whole hour has passed. It's this unintentional, mindless loss of time we want to help you avoid; where you're not even really enjoying what you're doing anyway. So let's get stuck in.

Time Magic Tricks for Unsucking Your Phone

We're going to start with simple tweaks you can make to your phone setup, and build up to behavioral shifts that can change your life.

BE RUTHLESS WITH YOUR APPS, ESPECIALLY SOCIAL MEDIA

Remove any apps you don't need. Be ruthless. Any app that encourages infinite usage can be particularly problematic, and social media apps are one of the biggest culprits — you can scroll forever, always finding something new, and always getting another hit of dopamine. For this reason, we've deleted all social media apps other than Instagram off our phones. So if we want to check the others we have to get on the computer. It's a small but meaningful step that adds "friction" to the process and makes it that little bit harder to get sucked in.

GET ORGANIZED

With the apps that remain on your phone, divide them into two categories:

1. **Non-social media apps**: These go on the first "page" of your phone. Create folders for your apps to house like with

like — for example, Photography, Health, Finance, Music, Education, Work, Travel — and drag your apps into the appropriate folder.

2. **Social media apps**: Put your social media apps in one folder on your phone, on the back page. Title this folder "Time Suckers" — this will hopefully make you think before you open that folder. On that note ...

TURN OFF ALL NOTIFICATIONS

Notifications stimulate the release of cortisol, your body's stress hormone. So those seemingly innocent "pings" when someone comments on your post or sends you a message are literally causing you stress — not cool! On top of the changes in brain chemistry, there's also a phenomenon scientists call "switching cost," which is what happens when you hear your phone ping, switch your attention away from the task at hand, then have to return to it afterwards. Not only does this pattern suck your time, it also affects your brain efficiency by up to 40 percent.[15] So the less your phone is able to destroy your attention with notifications, the better.

TURN YOUR PHONE ON SILENT OR AIRPLANE MODE

Our phones are always on silent unless we are waiting for an important call (which is hardly ever). We do this so we can choose when we respond to calls and messages.

SET AN AUTOMATIC TIME LIMIT

This is probably the single most important tip to reclaim control of your phone usage. In fact, of all the tips in this book, this one might just help you reclaim the most hours and the most "life" with the least amount of effort.

Step 1: Decide how long you want to spend on your phone each day. We want you to think deeply about it — how much time are you comfortable with donating to your phone and to social media companies each day?

Step 2: Double check your decision by looking at the *lifetime impact* of that amount. You'll need to do some simple math here:

+ Subtract your age from 79 to give you the average number of years left in your expected life span.
+ Multiply that number by 356, to give you the number of days you've got left.
+ Multiply that number by the amount you've chosen, expressed in hours, as a decimal. (So 15 minutes would be 0.25; 3 hours and 45 minutes would be 3.75.)
+ Now Google "hours to years calculator," plug in the number you reached, and see how many years it equates to. (Or if you prefer, you can do this step yourself: divide the number you've reached by 24, then again by 365.)

To see this in action, let's say you've chosen one hour per day, and you're 35 years old:

+ 79 − 35 = 44 years left of your expected average lifespan
+ 44 x 365 = 16,060 days left
+ 16,060 x 1 hour of phone usage = 16,060 hours phone usage over your lifetime.
+ Using an online "hours to years" calculator, 16,060 hours equates to 1.83 years of nonstop phone usage over your lifetime.

After doing this math, are you comfortable with giving that amount of your life to your phone and to social media platforms? Only you know the answer to that question. (One of our favorite quotes from Henry David Thoreau comes to mind here: "The price of anything is the amount of life you exchange for it.")

Step 3: Once you're happy with your chosen amount of phone time, go ahead and set up an **automatic time limit** on your phone usage. For iPhone users, the Screen Time app allows you to set limits on your overall phone time, and on the time you spend on specific apps. Android users can do the same within their Digital Wellbeing app. When you've hit your predetermined limit, your phone will display a warning note. This is your cue to come back to the present, realign with your life goals, and switch off your phone.

If you implement this step, and go from using your phone 4.8 hours per day (the average) to one hour per day (as in our example) you'll go from spending 12.8 years of your life on your phone, to 1.8 years.

That's 11 years of your life reclaimed.

And it's all yours.

Think of all the reading, or writing, or music making, or giggling, or connecting, or *whatever* you could do in 11 years — that's 4015 days, or 96,360 hours. Heck, you could complete two whole PhDs in that time!

This really is the most powerful time-reclaiming technique in the whole book, and it's so simple to action.

So please, if you take nothing else away from this book, let this one tip be the thing that sticks with you: setting an automatic cap on your screen time can literally change your life forever.

You're welcome ;)

ALLOW YOURSELF SPACE TO DO NOTHING

Way too many of us are trapped in the habit of using our phones (and, social media in particular) to fill up every spare moment of our lives. As soon as we have to sit idly and "do nothing" for more than a few seconds — whether at the dentist's office, in line at the grocery store, or even on the porcelain throne — the pull to reach for our phones is intense and often irresistible.

This habit can be a challenging one to break, but it's important to try. Those moments of white space are good for you — scratch that, they're *essential* for you. They allow your brain room to make new connections, to process your day, to cement long-term learning, to boost productivity, to build neurological flexibility, to clean out neurological waste products, and so much more.[16]

The best way we've found to reclaim space in your day for "nothingness" is to create "rules" for yourself around the places and situations where you simply do *not* use your phone, no matter what. These rules remove all choice or ambiguity from the situation, and make it easier in the moment to act in alignment with your personal values. Here are some ideas to get you started:

+ "I don't use my phone on the toilet."
+ "I don't use my phone while I'm in the bath."
+ "I don't use my phone while I'm boiling the kettle."
+ "I don't use my phone while I'm waiting for my kid at the school gate."
+ "I don't use my phone while I'm watching TV."

With personal boundaries like this in place, your phone stops being the default activity you reach for when you're in the bath or on the porcelain (!), and instead you can allow your mind some blissful space. Resist the urge to mentally compose a shopping list or stress about your to-do list, and instead, embrace the deliciousness of deliberate daydreaming. Far from being idle or lazy, you're actually doing something massively healthful and constructive for your brain.[17]

FIND A MEANINGFUL, ENGAGING REPLACEMENT FOR ALL YOUR SCROLL TIME

If you're serious about kicking your smartphone addiction, it's important to find something to replace all that scrolling. In Chapter 12, we're going to show you how to find and cultivate hobbies and activities that you're passionate about. For now, we want you to think seriously about what activities might be fun replacements for all those hours that are currently getting eaten up with mindless scrolling. Maybe you've been meaning to do more study? Or read more books? Or dust off your guitar? The only limit here is your imagination.

TIME MAGIC TRICK: FORWARD PLANNING YOUR PHONE-REPLACEMENT ACTIVITIES

If you haven't planned in advance what you want to do instead of phone time, it's all too easy to just fall back into the scroll trap (especially if you're tired after a long day, and your brainpower and willpower are at an ebb).

The solution is to plan *now* for what you'll do in those moments.

Write a list of activities you might like to explore instead of scrolling.

Here are some possibilities to get you started:

- Take a hot (or very cold) bath
- Do an art or craft activity
- Cook a new recipe
- Start a stretching or mobility routine
- Learn an instrument
- Go for a walk
- Give yourself a facial or dry body brush

- Plant an herb garden
- Write a song or poem
- Read a book
- Spend time connecting with your partner or kids
- Journal

Write down a minimum of 20 ideas. It might seem like a lot, but you need options to cover a wide range of moods and circumstances you might find yourself in.

When you're done, stick your list someplace where you'll see it. Then, in those moments when you have a block of time to fill and you feel the pull of your phone, consult this list, and commit to choosing and trying one of the activities for at least half an hour.

TAKE A "DIGITAL DAYCATION" EACH WEEK

Designate one day per week — we do Sundays, but whatever works for you — when you take a vacation from your phone. Essential calls and texts are fine, but nothing else. We really love this practice, and have found that it gives us a genuine mental "reset" that we've come to truly value and look forward to each week.

Troubleshooting

Whenever we talk about these strategies, we often encounter the same few questions from people, so we thought we'd address them here, in case you've been wondering the same things ...

"But my work requires me to be on call — I can't switch off the volume/notifications on my phone!"

There are plenty of instances where you might need to be on call — maybe you're a doctor or a doula, or maybe you have to be available to other team members in different time zones.

Whatever your situation, choose to look for the opportunities, not just the limitations, in your situation. Where can you set boundaries? Maybe you're on call every second week — so for that other week, practice exceptional digital hygiene and switch off all notifications and volume settings. Or maybe you need to be hyper-available during the week, but can set clear and firm boundaries around phone usage from 6 p.m. each night or on weekends.

If even that's not possible for you, and you need your phone with you a lot, maybe you need to get extra-strict about having no social media apps on your phone, so that at least when you're answering calls and texts, you're not also getting sucked down the social media rabbit hole at the same time.

Put simply, do what you can to make improvements that work with *your* unique lifestyle — they all add up and they all count.

"I can't turn my phone on silent: I need to be available for my kids/babysitter/sick aunt!"

We get it. When we're out and our daughter is home with our nanny, we definitely have our phones on (and not on silent mode) because we want to be available in case of an emergency.

That said, there are still workarounds for those times when you don't want to be interrupted except in case of said emergency.

In this instance, we suggest utilizing the "Do not disturb" function on your smartphone, which instantly silences all incoming calls and texts. (iPhone users: you'll find it in Settings > Focus > Do not disturb. If you see a little crescent moon in the corner of your screen, you'll know you've activated it correctly.)

When you're switching "Do not disturb" mode on, you'll see there are a number of settings you can play with, including having a list of "allowed" people whose phone calls and messages won't be silenced. Simply add in the phone number of your kid's school or your mum's mobile, and voilà — problem solved and focus maintained!

"But I can't give up social media, I need it for my work!"

Boy, do we understand!

We run a handful of businesses, and they all rely on social media. It's literally part of our jobs to be on these platforms: to interact with people, to post, to comment, to like, and to stay abreast of the latest trends.

But none of that precludes responsible usage of social media; none of it stops you from getting crystal clear on how much of your life you're willing to donate to these platforms.

Sure, if it's integral for your work, then you might need to settle for a higher number of total hours spent on social media. But you can still practice exquisite digital hygiene and exceptionally firm boundaries, just with your higher amount as the guideline.

The above suggestions are not meant to be "one size fits all" — you might need to do some tinkering to get things to fit for you.

But one thing we want to impress upon you is that for all the questions we've just answered here, there are workarounds available. All they required was a dollop of determination and a willingness to be creative.

We want to stress that even if your particular circumstances preclude you from making some of the changes we've suggested in this chapter, every step in the right direction counts. So don't think that just because you can't do things "perfectly" that there's no point taking action: there is. Especially when the benefits are so huge. Take this next point …

Breaking Your Phone Addiction Can Help You Live Longer

If all of the above still hasn't made you determined to create better digital habits, then consider this: putting down your phone can help you live longer.

We're going to look at the science of longevity in depth in Chapter 14, but we can't resist foreshadowing some of this hugely important topic here, in the context of your smartphone.

So far in this chapter, we've focused mainly on the addictive impact of smartphones and the way they trigger a cascade of dopamine in our brains, the neurotransmitter that can create addictive habits and behaviors.

But that's not the only neurotransmitter that's impacted by phone usage. Another one — which we've only mentioned briefly so far, but that potentially carries even more health risks — is cortisol.

Cortisol, if you recall, is the body's main stress hormone. It can be thought of as nature's "built-in alarm system."[18] It's perfectly natural and healthy to have cortisol in your system. In fact it's essential: if you encounter a dangerous situation — say, a mugger in a dark alley, or a grizzly bear in a forest — cortisol is one of the hormones that gets pumped into your bloodstream (along with others like adrenaline) that will help you run for your life and escape to safety. So it's a helpful hormone to have around!

What's *not* so helpful though, is when your cortisol levels become chronically elevated. Our bodies are designed to deal with *short-term* spikes of cortisol, where the danger passes quickly (the mugger runs off, the grizzly bear ambles away) and cortisol levels can drop, returning your body to its usual non-aroused state. The problem, though, is that our modern, fast-paced society can make our bodies and brains think that there's *always* danger around; that there's always a metaphorical grizzly bear chasing us. So our cortisol levels never get the chance to recede, they stay chronically spiked, and we end up feeling like we're in a permanent state of crisis — not exactly a fun way to live!

The plot twist that we're sure you've seen coming from a mile away is that **our phones are triggering that feeling of always being in crisis**. They are contributing to that flood of cortisol in our systems resulting in permanently elevated levels.[19] And it's hurting us.

All those pings, all that scrolling, all that content to keep up with — it's stressing us out! Not to mention all the ways in which our phone is disrupting our sleep, replacing our rest time, displacing our social connections, impacting our mental and physical health ... all of it adds up to one big cortisol surge that never seems to let up.

When you consider the vast number of serious and life-threatening health problems that stem from chronically elevated cortisol — including heart disease, stroke, diabetes, dementia, depression, anxiety, high blood pressure, mental illness, obesity, increased cholesterol, increased blood sugar, and increased inflammation[20] — the connection becomes clear: **our phones are quite literally hurting us and potentially shortening our lives.**

The good news is that everything we've already discussed in this chapter can help mitigate the nonstop cortisol surge and therefore reduce your risk of those negative health outcomes, theoretically helping you to live longer.

And just in case avoiding serious health issues and adding years to your life is still not enough motivation for you to address the digital drain, let's take a moment to consider the impact of smartphones on the tiny humans in your life.

Smartphones + Kids = An Equation We Can't Ignore

Did you know that the average "tween" spends less time outdoors than a prisoner?

Yep, as a rule, prisoners get to spend an hour outside each day. But a 2016 UK survey found that three out of four children spend under **60 minutes** playing outside each day — i.e., less time in nature than a prison inmate.[21] It's shocking, right?!

So what are our children doing with all this time that they're not outside? By and large, they're on screens.

The amount of time kids spend staring at a screen has risen at an alarming rate over the last 20 years. Research conducted in the UK in 2015 found that the average child aged between five and 16 spent **6.5 hours per day** glued to some sort of screen (tablet, mobile, television, video games, etc.).[22] Compare that to 20 years ago: in 1995, that figure was only around three hours per day. That's a staggering jump of 116 percent.[23]

Teenage boys were the highest screen users, averaging eight hours a day. (Eight!) That means that by the time they turn 20, our boys could easily have already spent *four whole years* of their lives on screens. That's 35,040 hours before they've even cut their twentieth birthday cake … um, WTF?!

It's no wonder then that children as young as 13 have reportedly entered rehab centers for "smartphone addiction." It's tricky enough to maintain responsible phone usage as fully grown adults, let alone as a kid with a still-developing brain. (A particularly impactful headline in *The Independent* summed up the situation with gut-dropping accuracy: "Giving your child a smartphone is like giving them a gram of cocaine, says top addiction expert.")[24]

So what on earth are parents supposed to do?

We are still figuring it out, and we don't have all the answers. But one thing we know for sure is that you have to lead by example. We all know there's no use telling your kids to eat broccoli while you're chowing down on chocolate cake. The exact same principle applies to your digital habits. If you care about teaching your child healthy digital habits, the best thing you can do is model healthy digital habits yourself, which makes the strategies in this chapter even more important. It's not just *your* time on the line, it's your children's. It's not just *your* life you're influencing, it's theirs. And how they spend their hours and their days will be influenced by how you spend *yours*.

It's a huge responsibility, we know. But you're reading this book, so we also know you're up to the task. You've got this. And if you ever need a gentle reminder (or a hefty kick in the tush) to take action and follow through on the strategies you find in these pages, this is surely it.

Now that you know how to reclaim a third of your waking hours, reduce the damaging effects of smartphone-induced cortisol surges and add years to your (and your child's) life by simply putting your phone down, let's home in on another major time-eater: emails.

Notes

1   www.bbc.com/news/technology-59952557
2   How did we get this figure? The average human life span is 79 years.
    So if someone is using their phone from age 15 to 79, that's 64 years x
    365 days x 4.8 hours/day = 112,128 hours = 12.8 years.
3   www.zdnet.com/article/americans-spend-far-more-time-on-their-
    smartphones-than-they-think/

4   theworldunplugged.wordpress.com/

5   Sadagopan A.P., Manivel R., Marimuthu A., Nagaraj H., Ratnam K., Krithikka R., Selvarajan L. and Genickson J., "Prevalence of Smart Phone Users at Risk for Developing Cell Phone Vision Syndrome among College Students," *Journal of Psychology and Psychotherapy* 7, 2017, doi: 10.4172/2161-0487.1000299

6   Gustafsson E., Thomée S., Grimby-Ekman A. and Hagberg M., "Texting on mobile phones and musculoskeletal disorders in young adults: A five-year cohort study," *Applied Ergonomics*, Volume 58, 2017, Pages 208–214, ISSN 0003-6870, doi.org/10.1016/j.apergo.2016.06.012

7   De-Sola Gutiérrez J., Rodríguez de Fonseca F. and Rubio G., "Cell-phone addiction: a review," *Frontiers in Psychiatry*, 2016; 7:175

8   Shoukat S., "Cell phone addiction and psychological and physiological health in adolescents," *EXCLI Journal*, February 2019, 4;18:47-50. PMID: 30956638; PMCID: PMC6449671

9   De-Sola Gutiérrez J, Rodríguez de Fonseca F, Rubio G., "Cell-phone addiction: a review," *Frontiers in Psychiatry* 2016; 7:175

10   Rosen L.D., Whaling K., Carrier L.M., Cheever N.A. and Rokkum J., "The media and technology usage and attitudes scale: an empirical investigation," *Computers in Human Behavior*, 2013; 29:2501–2511

11   *Ibid.*

12   Shoukat S., "Cell phone addiction and psychological and physiological health in adolescents," *EXCLI Journal*, February 2019; 4;18:47-50. PMID: 30956638; PMCID: PMC6449671

13   Ma, Z., Wang, J., Li, J. et al., "The association between obesity and problematic smartphone use among school-age children and adolescents: a cross-sectional study in Shanghai," *BMC Public Health*, 21, 2067 (2021). doi:10.1186/s12889-021-12124-6

14   Ward A.F., Duke K., Gneezy A. and Bos M.W., "Brain Drain: The Mere Presence of One's Own Smartphone Reduces Available Cognitive Capacity," *Journal of the Association for Consumer Research*, 2017 2:2, 140–154

15   www.apa.org/topics/research/multitasking

16   Immordino-Yang M.H., Christodoulou J.A., Singh V., "Rest Is Not Idleness: Implications of the Brain's Default Mode for Human Development and Education," *Perspectives on Psychological Science*, 2012 Jul; 7(4):352–64. doi: 10.1177/1745691612447308. PMID: 26168472

17   *Ibid.*

18   www.webmd.com/a-to-z-guides/what-is-cortisol

19   Afifi T.D., Zamanzadeh N., Harrison K. and Callejas M.A.,
     "WIRED: The impact of media and technology use on stress
     (cortisol) and inflammation (interleukin IL-6) in fast paced families,"
     Computers in Human Behavior, Volume 81, 2018, pp 265–273, ISSN
     0747-5632, doi.org/10.1016/j. chb.2017.12.010.; Chun J.W., Choi
     J., Cho H., Choi M.R., Ahn K.J., Choi J.S., Kim D.J., "Role
     of Frontostriatal Connectivity in Adolescents With Excessive
     Smartphone Use," *Front Psychiatry*, September 2018; 9:437. doi:
     10.3389/ fpsyt.2018.00437. PMID: 30258373; PMCID: PMC6143708

20   Jones C., Gwenin C., "Cortisol level dysregulation and its prevalence-
     Is it nature's alarm clock?" *Physiological Reports*, January 2021;
     8(24):e14644. doi: 10.14814/phy2.14644. PMID: 33340273; PMCID:
     PMC7749606

21   www.theguardian.com/environment/2016/mar/25/three-quarters-
     of-uk-children-spend-less-time-outdoors-than-prison-inmates-survey

22   www.bbc.com/news/technology-32067158

23   *Ibid.*

24   www.independent.co.uk/news/education/education-news/child-
     smart-phones-cocaine-addiction-expert-mandy-saligari-harley-street-
     charter-clinic-technology-teenagers-a7777941.html

CHAPTER 7

Email Emancipation

Ping, ping, ping …

Is that the sound of emails landing in your inbox? Or is it the sound of seven precious years of your life being hunted down and destroyed, never to be enjoyed again?

Trick question: it's both!

Email is a time-eater like no other. Unfortunately, many people aren't aware of how much life they're losing to their inbox, especially because dealing with emails gives us the illusion that we're engaging in an activity that's "useful," "meaningful," and "necessary." We hate to be the ones to break it to you but nine times out of ten, the opposite is true.

The two of us were losing so much of our lives to our inboxes that we decided to do something radical about it. Before we dig into the two revolutionary strategies we used, let's get super clear on precisely how much time the average person is losing to this hungry beast …

A survey conducted by software giant Adobe found that the

average US office worker spends just under three and a half hours per day checking their work email and another two hours and 23 minutes per day checking their personal email. That's nearly *six hours* of email-checking each day ... and the participants all said they expected this figure to increase over the coming years.[1]

That means a person entering the workplace today at age 20 and working through to the traditional retirement age of 65 can expect to spend more than 63,000 hours — or more than seven years of their life — on emails.[2]

If your jaw is on the floor right now, prepare yourself, because the cost of emails does not stop there ...

Research from the University of California Irvine suggests that the average time it takes to recover from a distraction — like checking an email — and return to the task at hand is 23 minutes and 15 seconds.[3] This means that every time you check your inbox, it's not just the time you spend reading or processing that email that's costing you, it's also the 23 minutes it takes you afterwards to get back to whatever it was you were supposed to be doing in the first place.

There's more. Check out this headline from CNN: "E-mails hurt IQ more than pot." Yep, email is damaging your IQ too! Clinical trials in the UK monitored the IQ of workers throughout the day. The data showed that workers who tried to juggle incoming emails with their work tanked their IQ by a whopping ten points. (To put that in context, that's the same drop experienced by people who miss an entire night of sleep, and more than double the four point drop that people experience after partaking of some — ahem — "greenery.")[4]

Now, we're not technophobes. Quite the opposite. So we'll freely admit that yes, there are benefits to email. Big ones. It's great to be able to shoot a message to someone on the other side of the world and have them respond within minutes. It's wonderful that we can send a whole group of people a message at once, without having to contact them individually. We even earn a significant portion of our income through email marketing.

So what's the answer? Is it possible to still reap the benefits of email, without exchanging seven years of your life in the process? We say yes, and we have a solution for you ... two of them, in fact!

Strategy 1: Creating Inbox Freedom

The goal of Inbox Freedom is a clear inbox each day, with all emails actioned in the fastest possible time, and with the most ease. (Stress and overwhelm have no place here!) This is the option Melissa has implemented in her work life, and it's a game changer.

To achieve this level of freedom, our preferred email provider is Gmail. We've used many, many email clients over the years, and nothing compares to Gmail. If you haven't got it yet, please consider getting it! We know you might be used to your current mail app, but the switch is so worth it. You can have your existing email account/s rerouted through your Gmail inbox, and you can send and receive mail from multiple addresses all within the one place (even if they're not Gmail addresses). We never looked back after making the switch, and we're guessing you won't either.

Once you've got your Gmail account set up ...

1. Decide when you would like to check your emails each day. Two to three dedicated sessions are more than enough. Melissa likes to check her email at 8.30 a.m. and 2.30 p.m., but you can do any schedule you like: 9 a.m., 12 p.m., and 4.30 p.m. is a popular set up for people who work "normal" business hours.

2. Schedule these times in your calendar each day. Depending on the volume of emails you receive, you may only need to block off a few minutes or it might be more.

3. Now here's the part that requires a bit of discipline but that makes all the difference: *do not let yourself check your inbox outside those allotted times.* Following through on this step might mean adjusting your workflow. For example, so many people keep their inbox open in a browser tab for their entire workday. Even if you've told yourself "I won't check it," it's far too tempting to your monkey brain to leave it there right in front of you. So shut it down, pronto!

4. Get "Boomerang for Gmail." This plugin is one of the best things ever. It lets you take control of when you send and receive email messages. There is a free version, but we use the paid one. With Boomerang, you can:

    a. **"Pause" your inbox**. With this setting on, new emails will be hidden from view until a predetermined time/s each day (which you can configure to align with your predetermined inbox check-in times). You can also ensure that all new emails received over a weekend stay hidden until Monday morning. This is an excellent setting to play around with, because it helps you maintain your commitment to limiting your email checks — and even if you do check, there'll be nothing there to see, which can help you break the habit. (You can "unpause" your inbox at any time, if you absolutely have to ... but you shouldn't need to!)

    b. **"Delay send" your emails**. Say you're answering emails on a weekend (for example, you might be about to jet off to Bali for a vacation, so you're doing some last-minute work before you switch off for a week). You can "delay send" those emails so that they don't actually get delivered until 9 a.m. on Monday morning (or any time that you specify). That way, your clients or colleagues never need to know you're working on a weekend, and they won't get the expectation that you'll respond outside of regular hours.

c. **"Boomerang" your incoming emails**. This genius plugin will return emails to your inbox (i.e., "boomerang" them) at a time you specify. Say you receive an email containing an event ticket that you won't need for another few weeks. With the click of a few buttons, Boomerang will archive the message (so it disappears from your inbox), then return it to your inbox when you need it. So useful, right?!

d. **"Boomerang" outgoing mail too**: Need to make sure you get a reply to a message you've sent? Boomerang will remind you if you haven't heard back within a specified timeframe. Again, it just takes a few clicks to configure your settings: "Boomerang this message in [a week/three days/tomorrow/etc.] if [no reply/not opened/not clicked/regardless]." This is awesome, because it means you can send an email, put it out of your mind, and if you haven't received a reply in the specified period, it jumps back to your inbox to remind you. This is the link to get Boomerang: www.boomeranggmail.com. (And remember, we don't get any kickbacks for recommending this app or any of the products we suggest in these pages. We just use and love them.)

Hot Tip: Gmail has a similar feature called "Snooze" which works very well in Boomerang's place. Best of all, it's free! But there is one extra step when using Snooze. When you compose a new email and hit send, you need to go to your Sent items and

Snooze it from there, much like you would use "Boomerang this message."

5. During your designated email sessions, for *every* email in your inbox, take one of the following five actions:

   a. Respond: Reply straight away (setting up a Boomerang reminder if you need to follow something up) then archive the message. (The blue "send and archive" button that you can turn on in Gmail allows you to do both these steps in one click. (#winning)

   b. Archive: If no response is needed, archive straight away.

   c. Delegate: Forward the email to someone in your team who can action it for you.

   d. Boomerang: Schedule the message to reappear in your inbox at a later date and time that is more convenient for you.

   e. Trash: Immediately bin any spam that's crept in!

By applying one of these five actions to every single email, you should have no problem achieving your goal of getting to inbox zero every day.

As you're applying these actions, don't second guess yourself. Move with speed and aim for swift decisions. Remember, when you're 80 years old and your time is getting more and more precious, you will *not* wish you spent more time on email!

The final step is to unsubscribe from any newsletters that no longer serve you. If you haven't opened a particular newsletter in the last two months, that's your sign: press that unsubscribe button, baby. It might take a chunk of time to go through and do this (especially if you've subscribed to a lot over the years) but once you've done it, you'll have a blissfully clutter-free inbox and you'll receive less mail moving forwards. #winning

These six steps are how Melissa created "inbox freedom." It's freed up so much time for her, and she'll never go back to the old way of doing things again.

Nick, on the other hand, was ready for something more revolutionary ...

NICK: THE CASE FOR NO EMAIL

I'm a maker at heart — music, documentaries, products, and more. A few years ago, I had a stark realization: the better I got at these things, the more my inbox was conspiring to keep me away from them.

At its worst, I was spending at least four hours a day on email. I'd sit down to clear out my inbox, and I'd only be halfway through my responses when new messages would start flooding in from the people I'd just replied to ... it felt like a losing battle! And to be honest, it was a battle I had no desire to fight.

So instead of coming up with a new system to tame my inbox inferno, I decided to do something truly revolutionary ... step out of the battle altogether.

Yep, I retired from email.

And it's been an absolute game changer for me, my work, my creativity, and my music.

Now, I'm going to say up front here that this option is not for everyone. But even if you can't retire from email entirely, perhaps my story and the following strategy will inspire you to step away from aspects of your inbox in whatever way you can.

Below is a brief overview of the steps I took. If you want the full play-by-play (including the exact job description I posted and more), check it out on www.TimeMagic.me.

Strategy 2: Retiring From Email

The process of retiring from email altogether goes like this:

1. CREATE A "STANDARD OPERATING PROCEDURE" (SOP) FOR MANAGING YOUR INBOX.

Wait until your inbox has built up for a few days. Then use a recording app to record yourself processing every single item in your inbox, explaining what you're doing and why you're doing it at every step. (We use Loom, a free plugin for Google Chrome that lets you record voice and video.) It might take you a few hours (or days, if your inbox is as bad as Nick's was!) to complete this task, but the more thorough you can be now, the easier your email retirement will be later.

2. HIRE AN "INBOX NINJA."

This is the person who will be managing your inbox. Note that you're not hiring someone to pretend to be you, just to think like you. Nick found his ninja on Upwork, an online marketplace for freelancers.

This whole strategy rests on hiring the right person, so be sure to interview prospective candidates carefully and thoroughly. It can also be prudent to set a few "test" tasks (paid, of course) for your top picks, to ensure that your future ninja has the right skillset, pays exceptional attention to detail and is a good personality fit for you.

3. SET UP A CATCH-ALL EMAIL ADDRESS.

Create a new catch-all email address which captures all your emails (work, personal, etc.) that you can then hand over to your ninja. Forward everything to the new address, so that all your mail is in one place.

4. TRAIN YOUR NINJA.

Once you've hired your ninja, have them watch the SOP video/s you created, so they can start learning how to think like you. You can also provide them with a spreadsheet full of "templates" for any responses you commonly send.

5. SET 'EM LOOSE!

Set your ninja loose inside your inbox, and let them start processing your emails. At first, they'll likely have lots of questions about how to deal with certain emails. But you'd be surprised by how quickly the right person can successfully take over this mammoth task and allow you to reclaim huge swathes of your life.

Nick's ninja processes his emails in a few ways: she actions what she can on her own, delegates items to other team members as needed, books things in his calendar, creates tasks for Nick directly in his Things app, and responds to emails (as herself, not as Nick). For the few messages that require Nick's input or personal response, she moves them all to a designated folder. Once a day, she sends Nick a voice message (via Voxer) to update him on anything important, ask him for guidance if there are any emails she's unsure of, or to let him know that he needs to action something in his folder.

With this revolutionary system in place, Nick spends about 5–10 minutes per day listening to voice messages from his ninja, and about 30–60 minutes per week in his inbox on the items that require his direct attention. Considering he went from four hours per day to less than one per week, you can safely say that his "retirement" has been a raging success! His time spent making music has gone up, the number of tracks he's released has shot through the roof, and he's also had significantly more time to spend with our kids.

When they hear Nick's story, people often comment that this must be an outrageously expensive solution. But an inbox ninja can be far more affordable than you may think. Ours started for around $40 per hour for a local (Australian) freelancer. She was so helpful to us (and created such huge value in our business) that we quickly asked her to come on board in an expanded capacity. We now call her our "Director of Everything" and couldn't live without her!

Whichever approach to email you use, know that you're going to experience amazing benefits … but only if you take action.

So let's do that, right here, right now. It's time to choose your path towards email emancipation. Maybe you want to create inbox freedom. Or maybe you want to be a retirement revolutionary.

Either way, by taking action, you should be able to easily halve the amount of time you spend in your inbox. That's a saving of 3.5 years of your life, which is a *lot* of life to reclaim.

So tell us, which one will you choose?

Once you've made your decision, it's time to switch gears because Part 3 is up next. And just quietly, it's where things start going stratospheric …

Notes

1 business.adobe.com/blog/perspectives/if-you-think-email-is-dead-think-again
2 How did we get this figure? The average worker spends five hours and 52 minutes (or 352 minutes) per day checking email. Over a 45 year career (working from age 20–65, 48 weeks per year, five days per week), that equates to 45 x 48 x 5 x 352 = 3,801,600 minutes = 63,360 hours = 7.2328767 calendar years.
3 www.ics.uci.edu/gmark/chi08-mark.pdf
4 edition.cnn.com/2005/WORLD/europe/04/22/text.iq/

PART THREE

Time Magic and You

Now that you know how to *save* time, the question becomes: **How can you make the most of your time?** The answer lies in optimizing all the important areas of your life — including your health, headspace, wealth, and work — so that you're operating at your peak, hitting your full potential and poised to squeeze every ounce of goodness out of the time available to you. Read on to discover: an ancient technique that will literally slow down your experience of time, a simple activity that can improve your time management by a whopping 72 percent, why it's so crucial to "know your numbers," how "subscription creep" is sending us into debt, the daily routine that can help keep you sprightly well into your twilight years, and how the greatest magic trick of all is to do work you love.

CHAPTER 8

Health Hacks

The Bugatti Chiron Super Sport is one of the fastest cars in the world. Boasting sophisticated design, innovative technology, and a 16-cylinder engine, this aerodynamic automobile can rip around a racetrack in a record 489 kilometers per hour. (If you'd like to own one, you'll have to get in line — there were only 30 of these bad boys made, and they retail for a cool $5.8 million apiece.)

But we're not here to praise the Bugatti's superlative engineering, its extra horsepower, or even its off-the-charts speed capability. What we want to point out is this: even though it's one of the most advanced vehicles in the world, if you don't put fuel in it, the Bugatti Chiron Super Sport won't go.

Anyone who's owned a car knows this. Owners of high-performance sports cars like the Bugatti Chiron Super Sport know something extra: if you want your car to perform at its peak and reach its full potential, it's not enough to just fuel it up; you also need to optimize the way its internal systems work.

If you think we're about to tell you that your body is like the Bugatti Chiron Super Sport, we're not. Your body is way more advanced, intelligent, complex, sophisticated, innovative, specialized, precious, and cutting-edge than that. The highest tech car in the world is still no match for a single cell of the human body, and your body is made up of trillions of cells.

Still, the car analogy is useful: if you want your body to "go," to perform at its peak, and to last, you need to take care of and optimize all its parts and systems.

Luckily, that's a lot simpler than it may sound. In this chapter, we're going to walk you through the eight health hacks that we believe are the highest-impact techniques you can use to uplevel your health. Then in Chapter 14, we'll be showing you how to make your engine "last."

Now, these health hacks you're about to read are worthwhile and valuable in their own right, but you might still have a very valid question: **why on earth are we talking about health in a book about time?!**

Our answer is simple: anyone who's talking about how to maximize time while ignoring health is missing a crucial piece of the puzzle. When your body and mind are healthy and functioning at their peak:

+ You'll have more energy to channel into your work, your hobbies, your loved ones, your creative pursuits, and more
+ You'll be more able to focus and avoid distraction
+ You'll feel better inside your own skin
+ You'll be stacking the odds in your favor for long-term health, strength, mobility, flexibility, endurance, and more
+ Your time management improves by up to 72 percent.

And that's just for starters.

Before we dive in, we want to preface this chapter with two important points. Firstly, you may already be familiar with some of these hacks. But it is one thing to know something and another to truly practice and embody that knowledge.

Secondly, becoming a true Time Magic master means pulling the levers that deliver the greatest impact. This means that some of the following recommendations may sound simple or basic. But in our experience, the lowest hanging fruit is the ripest, and it's often the "basics" that yield the biggest results.

So with that in mind, let's look at the steps you can take today to set yourself up for outrageously epic health, both now and for the long haul.

Time Magic Health Hack 1: Food as Fuel

You can bet that anyone who owns a fancy sports car is only putting the best possible fuel in their vehicle. And remember, your body is a zillion times more sophisticated and special than any vehicle. So it's worth considering: what kind of fuel are you feeding yours?

We know that the topic of food and nutrition can seem like a minefield, with different people saying different things at any given moment. We also know it can be overwhelming to try to sift through all that noise, especially when so much of it is contradictory and always changing when all you really want to know is: "What the heck should I put in my mouth?!"

The Time Magic approach to food is simple: eat real, whole foods from Mother Nature, focusing mainly on plants. That's it!

There are plenty of nutrition fads that might tempt you to stray from this approach. You might read an article trumpeting: "Butter is bad!" (followed one week later, of course, by an article declaring: "Butter is back!"). But who's got time for all that back-and-forth?! While the noisy mob debates the merits of butter or beef or whatever food *du jour* has made it into the headlines this week, why not stick with the foods that have been shown time and time again to help your body thrive?

Numerous studies have shown the massive array of benefits of a plant-based lifestyle, with demonstrated positive impact on obesity, diabetes, heart disease, high blood pressure, and overall mortality among others.[1]

These studies are hugely persuasive. It's also interesting to look at which diet has been proven to help humans live longer, and there's plenty of evidence that centenarians — aka people who've reached the age of 100 — eat diets that are high in plants, and importantly, include a high amount of diversity.[2] (More on this in Chapter 14.)

Even with this overwhelming body of evidence, there's another reason why we love eating this way (and it's not just that it makes us feel amazing).

After ten-plus years of working with people to help them become their best selves via podcasts, programs, products, documentaries, apps, coaching, and more, one thing that we've noticed is that people are more likely to succeed at making change in their lives — and crucially, at sustaining that change — when the changes they make are simple.

So the fact that this way of eating combines a whole host of health benefits with elegant simplicity is a win-win in our book.

The truth is, you can't go wrong with a plate built around whole, plant-based foods including vegetables; fruit; legumes, pulses; nuts and seeds; mushrooms; and herbs and spices. So embrace what Mother Nature has to offer, do what the centenarians do, and fill your kitchen, your plate, and your belly with an abundance of whole plant foods.

Time Magic Health Hack 2: Drink More Water

Did you know that your body is made up of around 60 percent water?[3]

All that water inside you isn't just sloshing around, it's working hard! It performs a number of functions, including:

+ Carrying nutrients to your cells
+ Removing waste from your body (e.g., through urine and sweat)
+ Maintaining joint health, cushioning, and lubrication
+ Protecting sensitive tissues like the spinal cord
+ Aiding digestion
+ Preventing constipation
+ Maintaining balance of electrolytes
+ Regulating your temperature.[4]

With so many important functions to take care of, even slight dips of 1–2 percent in hydration levels can have a big impact on how you feel and perform throughout the day.[5] That's why it's so crucial to stay hydrated.

There's actually very little science on how much water we need to function optimally, but the general rule of thumb for an adult is to have eight glasses of water per day — and more if you are run down, unwell, exercising, pregnant, or breastfeeding. If you need to, set a reminder in your phone to make sure you're regularly having a swig.

TIME MAGIC TRICK: DRINK UP FOR BETTER MOOD AND CONCENTRATION

Studies show that even a 1 percent fluid loss can impact working memory, mood and concentration, and can result in cognitive impairment, headaches, fatigue and anxiety.[6]

So the next time you're sitting at your desk and can't seem to concentrate, or you're feeling cranky or suffering from brain fog, try reaching for a big glass of water and feel your brain performance perk right back up again ... what a huge win for such a simple trick!

Once you've optimized the amount of water you drink, you can also optimize the quality of that water. If you have the resources, consider installing a filter on your taps or even better, a whole-house water filtration system. Also pay attention to the kind of water bottle you use when you're drinking on the go. We love our glass bottles but stainless steel is also a great option, especially for kids.

Time Magic Health Hack 3: Move Your Body

You've heard it before. In fact, maybe you've heard it so many times that this health hack might even make you roll your eyes: "Yeah guys, I know I should exercise." But there's a good reason why this advice has been repeated so many times it's now a cliché — because it's so incredibly good for you!

In 2015, the Academy of Medical Royal Colleges in the UK called exercise a "miracle cure"[7] and we wholeheartedly agree.

We love movement and exercise so much, we could fill this whole chapter with nothing but bullet points about all the incredible benefits it gives you. Instead, we'll limit ourselves to the following handful. Did you know that exercise can help prevent:

+ Cancer
+ Cardiovascular disease
+ Depression
+ Diabetes
+ High blood pressure
+ Joint and bone disease
+ Obesity
+ Osteoporosis
+ And premature death.[8]

Not too shabby, right?!

But here's the thing: you know by now that this book is different from other books you've read in the past. So we're not going to repeat the same information you've heard dozens of times before (you're a smart cookie. You already know exercise is good for you). Instead we want to reframe movement for you, and show you the huge effect it can have on your performance in other areas of your life, such as your ability to perform optimally in your work, enjoy your leisure time to the fullest, elevate your creative reasoning and engage in fun activities with your loved ones.

So with that in mind, consider the following:

+ Exercise has been shown to improve time management at work by a whopping 72 percent.[9]
+ Exercise significantly improves work performance and rate of task completion.[10]
+ High intensity functional exercise can improve your attention span.[11]

+ Walking can skyrocket your creativity by 81 percent, help you have better ideas, and help you break through creative lulls.[12]
+ Short-term exercise gives you a big-time brain boost. Even just a one-off ten-minute exercise session can boost your brain performance, focus, and problem solving by 14 percent.[13]

We could go on, but you get the picture. In short, exercise might just be one of the most powerful tools at your disposal when it comes to improving your work performance and your creativity, along with your focus, time management, problem-solving and more.

We'll be sharing an easy-to-follow customizable exercise plan in Chapter 14, but for now, if you're someone who struggles to get moving or to stay consistent with exercise, here are our top tips:

+ **Find something you enjoy doing and movement will become a source of true pleasure.** Put another way: if you don't enjoy exercise, you haven't found the right activity yet. Keep trying things until you find one you enjoy. It doesn't matter what it is — dancing, yoga, hiking, gardening, lawn bowls, ultimate Frisbee, whatever! The most important factor is that it gets you moving and that you like doing it.
+ **Make it simple.** You don't need a heap of fancy equipment, or a gym membership, or anything, really, to reap the benefits of exercise. Walking is one of the simplest activities on the planet (and one of our personal favorite types of movement) and all you need is a safe area to start strutting. You don't even need shoes if you want to make like a caveman and go barefoot. Body-weight exercise (including planks, squats, sit-ups, push-ups, and lunges) are also extremely effective and require zero equipment.

+ **Short sessions pack a punch.** Don't underestimate the power of a short burst of exercise. On days when you really don't feel like training, commit to moving your booty for just five to ten minutes. Even that short amount of time will give you a boost, and you'll often find that you want to continue for longer than you first planned.

To be honest, movement isn't something we have to "work" at including in our lives because we both love it so much and know how much better we feel when we do it. But it wasn't always that way. So if you're struggling to enjoy exercise right now, just know that it truly can become something that you want to do, not that you have to force yourself to do. Stick with it, start small, and see the huge benefits stack up … you'll never look back.

TIME MAGIC MASTER: JAMES WILKS

To say that James Wilks is an overachiever is an understatement. He's an MMA (mixed martial arts) fighter, winner of the Ultimate Fighter competition, an elite Special Forces trainer, and also the producer and star of the documentary *The Game Changers*. He's also one of the most inspiring people we know. When we asked him what his #1 Time Magic Trick was, here's what he said:

"For me, it's really important to be physically active, for both physical and mental health but also just to feel great.

"For a lot of people, including myself, it's sometimes hard to carve out the time to train. Part of my workout routine includes going to the gym and lifting weights. When I was younger, I could have been in the gym for an hour and a half, or even up to two hours. These days it's usually around 30–45 minutes, but I actually get better results. This is for two main reasons:

1. I primarily choose "compound" exercises, those that work multiple muscle groups at the same time, over "isolation" exercises, movements that target a specific muscle group and make use of only one joint.

2. Rather than taking a long rest period before each set, these days I do a lot more of what are known as "super sets," i.e., performing a set of two different exercises back-to-back with minimal rest in between. These are almost always "opposite" types of exercise. For example, I would do one pushing exercise (e.g., landmine press) followed promptly by a pulling exercise (e.g., one arm cable row) and then go back and forth for five sets of each (two warm-up sets and three heavy working sets). While I need time for one set of muscles to rest in between sets, my body overall doesn't need to rest. Muscles in exercise A are resting while doing exercise B and vice versa. I then repeat that concept with a few different pairs of exercises.

"If I'm really busy and don't have time to leave the house, I'll get in the garage and see how many body-weight squats, push-ups and pull-ups I can do in a given time. Even 10 or 20 minutes is a great workout, hitting major muscle groups with all three exercises being compound. Again here, I "super set." Personally, I do 30 squats, 20 push-ups, and 10 pull-ups, and then repeat. If this is too tough on any of the exercises, one can drop the numbers in each set. Additionally, one can modify the exercises if they are too challenging. Partial squats, knee push-ups, and rows with a workout band can all be substitutes.

"If physical activity is a priority for you, you'll find the time in your schedule to fit it in!"

TIME MAGIC TRICK: STAND UP TO LEVEL UP

Sitting is the new smoking ... or so the saying goes!

Both our chiropractor and our osteopath say that they're treating more people than ever before whose problems all stem from sitting. In fact, they told us that 90 percent of their clients' issues are sitting-related.

If that's not reason enough to get you off your tush, maybe these nuggets will:

One peer-reviewed study found that people who stood more often and for extended periods throughout the day had healthier brains — in particular, they showed less wear and tear on their temporal lobes.[14]

Another study showed that standing up in the classroom significantly increased focus, executive function, and memory in students.[15]

Standing up while working was shown to reduce mental fatigue, improve job performance, and increase employee engagement, according to a study published in the *British Medical Journal*.[16]

Melissa

I'm a huge fan of standing up to work. If you want to give this a try, you don't need an expensive purpose-built desk or other fancy equipment. Right now, as I write this, I have my laptop on top of a stack of books set at the perfect height.

You also don't need to stand for extended periods to get benefits. In fact, the research shows that a mixture of sitting and standing is best, as prolonged standing can result in joint aches, discomfort, and fatigue.[17]

Try starting with 20–30 minute blocks and build up to an hour. You'll notice the difference — not just in your spine and tush, but in your work performance as well.

Time Magic Health Hack 4:
Stretch Your Body

You might not think about flexibility much, but it pervades everything — if you want to sit at a computer, run around with your dog, crawl around with your kid, climb up a ladder, and sleep soundly at night, and you want to do those things without pain, your body needs to be flexible.

And if you want to continue doing all those things in your seventies and beyond, then your body needs to be *really* flexible.

From a Time Magic perspective, stretching is incredibly important. Whether your work is active (yoga teacher, carpenter, dancer) or sedentary (sitting at a desk or computer all day), if you can't get through your work without stiffness and joint pain, it will be hard to perform at your peak. You'll also struggle to fully enjoy your leisure activities and hobbies, and it will only get worse as you age (numerous studies show that flexibility decreases as we age, sometimes at an alarmingly fast rate!).[18]

Luckily, a dedicated stretching practice can increase the range of motion in your limbs, and can be a pleasant and enjoyable addition to your daily routine. It will also help to keep you spritely well into your twilight years.

Our own stretching routine relies heavily on yoga — a practice that we've both loved for decades, that has improved our flexibility out of sight, and that's offered numerous other benefits to boot. If you're not sure where to start, you'll find plenty of guided yoga or general stretching routines online. You'll feel the difference after even just a few minutes per day — sneak it in while watching TV, or chatting with your spouse, or on the phone with a friend!

Time Magic Health Hack 5: Focus on Fascia

There's a body part that you might not even know you have, that can play a huge role in how well you feel and move in your daily life. It's called fascia. It's the thin, filmy layer of white connective tissue that sits underneath your skin, forming a sheath around every muscle and organ in your body. (If you're picturing your muscles and organs wrapped in shrink-wrap, you're on the right track!)

For a long time, western medicine didn't understand the importance of fascia. It was thought to be inert, uninteresting, and of so little consequence that it was largely ignored. It was literally peeled off and discarded during autopsies, so that researchers could get to the "important" stuff underneath!

Nowadays, though, we know that fascia is incredibly important, and we're learning more and more about its impact in the body every day. It's now accepted that fascia plays important roles when it comes to physical movement, alignment and posture, range of motion, muscle stiffness, and fluid flow throughout the body. Its reach may be even wider than that, with researchers investigating its potential involvement in conditions as varied and unexpected as cancer, chronic fatigue, lymphedema, immune dysfunction, and gastrointestinal issues.[19] Whatever we come to learn in the years ahead (and you can bet that our eyes will remain firmly fixed on the research coming out in this area) for now, there's no doubt that keeping your fascia healthy, flexible, and supple is going to help optimize your performance, both when it comes to movement (whether that's running a marathon or picking up your kids/fur baby) and static poses (like sitting at your desk or standing up with proper alignment).

Our favorite fascia fix is foam rolling. Many people think of foam rollers as a "gimmick" or as something that "only elite athletes use," but there is so much more to them than that, and we believe that pretty much everyone can benefit from getting their roll on.

A foam roller works in a similar way to a rolling pin rolling out dough. You might start with a ball of stiff, lumpy dough that's not smooth or pliable at all. But once you start rolling it out, your dough becomes flexible and supple, and you can start doing and making all sorts of things with it. (Cookies, anyone?!) Likewise, foam rolling smooths out your fascia, flushing it with fresh blood, hydrating and oxygenating it, resulting in reduced knots and stiffness plus increased range of motion and flexibility.

We also love foam rollers for their relaxation benefits. After a day on your feet, lying on a foam roller (either with the roller aligned vertically with your spine and your arms splayed out either side in a "T" shape, or with the roller running horizontally across your back where a bra strap would go) is incredibly relaxing and calming for your nervous system.

There are loads of free videos online that will show you how to foam roll, so have a search. (Try specifying the body area you'd most like to release, such as "Tight shoulders and foam rolling routine.")

Also worth noting: it won't take you long to see benefits — one study found that just 90 seconds to two minutes of foam rolling was enough for participants to feel relief and see significant improvements in range of motion.[20] (Again, it's another huge win with a minimum of effort!)

So get rolling, do it daily, and feel the difference in your body and mind. And, much like stretching, this is the perfect activity to do while listening to a podcast, chatting to a friend, etc.

Time Magic Health Hack 6: Optimize Your Sleep

We spend 26 years of our life sleeping — more time than we'll devote to any other activity in our lives. And yet most people aren't attempting to optimize those 26 years — which, as far as we're concerned, means that you're missing out on some low-hanging fruit that can seriously upgrade your health, your performance, how you feel each day, and so much more.

Here are our best-ever tips for radically improving your sleep:

TIME MAGIC SLEEP TRICKS

1. Get off your phone and other devices at least two hours before you want to go to bed. Smartphones and devices wreak havoc on your sleep — the blue light they emit interrupts your circadian rhythms, they stimulate your brain and they can cause a surge of cortisol (and let's face it: a jolt of stress hormones right before bed is the exact opposite of what we want!). Seriously, if there's only one tip from this list that you take action on, make it this one. And if you absolutely must look at a screen for some reason, wear blue-blocking glasses to reduce the impact on your sleep.

2. Remove all tech from your bedroom. In particular, don't sleep with your phone charging next to you — it's way too tempting to reach over and start scrolling late at night or first thing in the morning. If you usually use your phone as a clock or an alarm, go old-school and get an analog one instead.

3. In the morning, try to get bright, natural light on your eyeballs within 30–60 minutes of waking. This triggers a

neural circuit which ensures you get sleepy at the correct time that evening and also improves the quality of your sleep.[21]

4. Ensure your room is as quiet and dark as possible. Wear earplugs and an eye mask if you need to, or consider blackout blinds.

5. Set your bedroom to the ideal temperature. Most researchers agree that a slightly cool room is ideal for deep sleep — around 18 degrees Celsius (65 degrees Fahrenheit).

6. Reduce your EMF (electric and magnetic fields) exposure by turning off your Wi-Fi at night or putting it on an automatic timer. Better yet, don't have Wi-Fi at all and hardwire your computer and TV into the wall (that's what we do).

7. Try not to drink or eat late in the evening, so that your stomach isn't forced to digest a heavy meal at the same time as you're trying to go to sleep. Aim to finish eating at least two hours before you hop in the cot. Get your water in earlier in the day too. For us, if we drink too late in the day we will almost always need to wake in the night to go to the bathroom. If that's you too, reduce your liquids in the late afternoon and evening and see if it helps.

Time Magic Health Hack 7: Get Enough Vitamin D

Despite its name, vitamin D is not actually a vitamin at all, it's a prohormone. It's the "nosy neighbor" of the body — sticking its beak into just about everything that's going on in the body. It's involved in so many processes and outcomes, including bone strength, muscle strength and immunity, as well as the creation of disease-preventing enzymes and proteins. It also affects the expression of thousands of genes. To say it's an "all-rounder" is an understatement!

Unfortunately, large swathes of the population don't get enough of this powerhouse prohormone — vitamin D deficiency is thought to be one of the most common medical conditions worldwide.[22] This can lead to all kinds of health problems including poor bone development, and increased risk of autoimmune disease, cardiovascular disease, diabetes, and common cancers.[23] Vitamin D can be found in foods like red meat, oily fish, liver, and egg yolks, although it's very difficult to get all your requirements from food alone.

Luckily, there's another source that's easily available and totally free, and you'll find it right outside your front door: the sun. Getting a healthy dose of sunlight on your bare skin stimulates your body to produce vitamin D and can help you meet your optimal daily requirements. How much time you'll need to spend in the sun depends on your unique skin, where you live, and what season it is. (If you live in the far northern or southern regions of the globe, during the winter months you may have to look to supplementation to meet your daily requirements. A whole year's supply costs about as much as a few coffees, so this is a very affordable way to ensure your bases are covered.)

Of course, too much sun exposure comes with its own risks, so take a sensible approach: don't overdo it and never let yourself get burnt.

While you're outside soaking up those rays, you'll also be getting a host of other benefits too, so let's talk about those ...

Time Magic Health Hack 8: Get Outside!

If there was a pill you could take that:

+ Decreased the level of stress hormones (like cortisol and adrenaline) circulating in your body
+ Increased the activity of your body's natural anti-cancer cells
+ Reduced blood pressure
+ Reduced heart rate
+ Improved mood
+ Reduced anxiety
+ Reduced depression
+ Decreased anger
+ Decreased fatigue
+ Decreased confusion
+ Increased energy and vigor
+ Activated your parasympathetic nervous system
+ Prevented numerous lifestyle-related diseases

… and if that pill had no side effects and no risks, can you imagine how many pharmaceutical companies would be clamoring to trademark the rights, manufacture it by the crap-ton, then charge you an exorbitant price for it?

The thing is, there *is* something that gives you all those incredible benefits, that doesn't have any downsides, and that's actually free: time in nature. Yep, spending time outdoors gives you all those benefits and more.[24]

Most of the published research in this area focuses on the benefits of time spent in forests (known as *shinrin-yoku* or "forest bathing" in Japan) and near bodies of water like the ocean. But any time in nature has proven benefits, even if it's just walking around the tiny patch of grass at the end of your street, or sitting next to the pots of herbs on your balcony.

While exercising outdoors is a great way to get some nature time (and kill two Time Magic Health Hacks with one stone!), it's not necessary to break a sweat to soak up Mother Nature's goodness — it's enough to simply *be* in nature. So get that tush outside and start reaping those incredible benefits, stat!

So there you have it: our eight favorite Time Magic Health Hacks. Put these into practice and you'll have all your bases covered when it comes to optimizing how your body functions. Then you can move on to optimizing another hugely important part of your health: your brain.

Notes

1   Berkow S.E., Barnard N., "Vegetarian diets and weight status," *Nutrition Reviews*, April 2006; 64(4):175–188. DOI: dx.doi. org/10.1111/j.1753-4887.2006.tb00200.x; Farmer B., Larson B.T., Fulgoni V.L., 3rd, Rainville A.J., Liepa G.U., "A vegetarian dietary pattern as a nutrient-dense approach to weight management: an analysis of the national health and nutrition examination survey 1999–2004," *Journal of the American Dietetic Association*, June 2011; 111(6):819–827. DOI: dx.doi.org/10.1016/j.jada.2011.03.012; *J Obes* (Lond) 2009 Jun;33(6):621–628; Snowdon D.A., Phillips R.L., "Does a vegetarian diet reduce the occurrence of diabetes?," *American Journal of Public Health*, May 1985 May; 75(5):507–12. DOI: dx.doi.org/10.2105/AJPH.75.5.507; Barnard N.D., Cohen J., Jenkins D.J., et al., "A low-fat vegan diet improves glycemic control and cardiovascular risk factors in a randomized clinical trial in individuals with type 2 diabetes," *Diabetes Care*, August 2006; 29(8):1777–83. DOI: dx.doi. org/10.2337/dc06-0606; Ornish D., Brown S.E., Scherwitz L.W., et al., "Can lifestyle changes reverse coronary heart disease? The Lifestyle Heart Trial," *The Lancet*, July 1990, 21; 336(8708):129–133. DOI: dx.doi.

org/10.1016/0140-6736(90)91656-U; de Lorgeril M., Salen P., Martin J.L., Monjaud I., Delaye J. and Mamelle N., "Mediterranean diet, traditional risk factors, and the rate of cardiovascular complications after myocardial infarction: final report of the Lyon Diet Heart Study," *Circulation*, February 1999; 99(6):779–85. DOI: dx.doi. org/10.1161/01. CIR.99.6.779; Agriculture Research Service US Department of Agriculture, US Department of Health and Human Services, *Report of the Dietary Guidelines Advisory Committee on the dietary guidelines for Americans to the Secretary of Agriculture and the Secretary of Health and Human Services*, Washington, DC, May 2010; Takahashi Y., Sasaki S., Okubo S., Hayashi M. and Tsugane S., "Blood pressure change in a free-living population-based dietary modification study in Japan," *Journal of Hypertension*, March 2006; 24(3):451–8. DOI: dx.doi.org/10.1097/01. hjh.0000209980.36359.16; Sinha R., Cross A.J., Graubard B.I., Leitzmann M.F., Schatzkin A., "Meat intake and mortality: a prospective study of over half a million people," *International Archives of Internal Medicine*, March 2009, 23;169(6):562–571. DOI: 10.1001/archinternmed.2009.6

2   Longo V.D. and Anderson R.M., "Nutrition, longevity and disease: From molecular mechanisms to interventions," *Cell*, 2022; 185 (9): 1455. DOI: 10.1016/j.cell.2022.04.002

3   www.medicalnewstoday.com/articles/what-percentage-of-the-human-body-is-water

4   www.medicalnewstoday.com/articles/what-percentage-of-the-human-body-is-water#calculation; www.health.harvard.edu/staying-healthy/how-much-water-should-you-drink

5   Ayotte D. and Corcoran M.P., "Individualized hydration plans improve performance outcomes for collegiate athletes engaging in in-season training," *Journal of the International Society of Sports Nutrition*, June 2018, 15(1):27. doi: 10.1186/s12970-018-0230-2. PMID: 29866199; PMCID: PMC5987390

6   *Ibid.;* Ganio M.S., Armstrong L.E., Casa D.J., McDermott B.P., Lee E.C., Yamamoto L.M., Marzano S., Lopez R.M., Jimenez L., Le Bellego L., Chevillotte E. and Lieberman H.R., "Mild dehydration impairs cognitive performance and mood of men," *British Journal of Nutrition*, 2011, 106(10), 1535-1543. doi: 10.1017/ S0007114511002005

7   www.aomrc.org.uk/wp-content/uploads/2016/05/Exercise_the_Miracle_Cure_0215.pdf

8   Warburton D.E., Nicol C.W., Bredin S.S., "Health benefits of physical activity: the evidence," *Canadian Medical Association Journal*, March 2006;174(6):801-9. doi: 10.1503/cmaj.051351. PMID: 16534088; PMCID: PMC1402378

9   Coulson J.C., McKenna J. and Field M., "Exercising at work and self-reported work performance," *International Journal of Workplace Health Management*, 2008, Vol. 1 No. 3, pp. 176–197. doi: 10.1108/17538350810926534

10 *Ibid.*

11 Ben-Zeev T., Hirsh T., Weiss I., Gornstein M., Okun E., "The Effects of High-intensity Functional Training (HIFT) on Spatial Learning, Visual Pattern Separation and Attention Span in Adolescents," *Frontiers in Behavioral Neuroscience*, September 2020, 14:577390. doi: 10.3389/ fnbeh.2020.577390. PMID: 33093827; PMCID: PMC7521200

12 Oppezzo M. and Schwartz D.L., "Give Your Ideas Some Legs: The Positive Effect of Walking on Creative Thinking," *Journal of Experimental Psychology: Learning, Memory, and Cognition*, 2014, Vol. 40, No. 4, 1142–1152

13 University of Western Ontario, "Short-term exercise equals big-time brain boost: Even a one-time, brief burst of exercise can improve focus, problem-solving." *ScienceDaily*, 21 December 2017, www. sciencedaily.com/releases/2017/12/171221122543.htm

14 Siddarth P., Burggren A.C., Eyre H.A., Small G.W., Merrill D.A., "Sedentary behavior associated with reduced medial temporal lobe thickness in middle-aged and older adults," *PLOS ONE*, 2018, 13(4): e0195549. doi.org/10.1371/journal.pone.0195549

15 Mehta R., Shortz A. and Benden M., "Standing Up for Learning: A Pilot Investigation on the Neurocognitive Benefits of Stand-Biased School Desks," *International Journal of Environmental Research and Public Health*, 2015; 13 (2): 59. DOI: 10.3390/ ijerph13010059

16 Edwardson C.L., Yates T., Biddle S.J.H., Davies M.J., Dunstan D.W., Esliger D.W. et al., "Effectiveness of the Stand More AT (SMArT) Work intervention: cluster randomised controlled trial," *British Medical Journal*, 2018; 363 :k3870. doi: 10.1136/bmj.k3870

17 Baker R., Coenen P., Howie E., Lee J., Williamson A. and Straker L. "A detailed description of the short-term musculoskeletal and cognitive effects of prolonged standing for office computer work,"

Ergonomics, 2018, 61:7, 877–890, DOI. 10.1080/00140139.2017.1420825

18 Stathokostas L., Little R.M., Vandervoort A.A., Paterson D.H., "Flexibility training and functional ability in older adults: a systematic review," *Journal of Aging Research*, 2012; 2012:306818. doi: 10.1155/2012/306818. Epub 2012 Nov 8. PMID: 23209904; PMCID: PMC3503322

19 Stecco A., Stern R., Fantoni I., De Caro R., Stecco C., "Fascial Disorders: Implications for Treatment," *PM&R Journal*, 2016, Volume 8, Issue 2, pp 161–168, ISSN 1934-1482,(www.sciencedirect.com/science/article/pii/ S1934148215002920); www.newscientist.com/article/mg25433861- 200-fascia-the-long-overlooked-tissue-that-shapes-your-health/

20 Hendricks S., Hill H., den Hollander S., Lombard W., Parker R., "Effects of foam rolling on performance and recovery: A systematic review of the literature to guide practitioners on the use of foam rolling," *Journal of Bodywork and Movement Therapies*, 2020, Volume 24, Issue 2, 2020, pp 151-174, ISSN 1360- 8592, doi.org/10.1016/j.jbmt.2019.10.019

21 Figueiro, M.G. et al., "The impact of daytime light exposures on sleep and mood in office workers," *Sleep Health: Journal of the National Sleep Foundation*, Volume 3, Issue 3, 204-215

22 Hovsepian S., Amini M., Aminorroaya A., Amini P., Iraj B., "Prevalence of vitamin D deficiency among adult population of Isfahan City, Iran," *Journal of Health, Population and Nutrition*, April 2011, 29(2):149– 55. doi: 10.3329/jhpn.v29i2.7857. PMID: 21608424; PMCID: PMC3126987

23 Holick M.F., "Vitamin D deficiency," *New England Journal of Medicine*, 2007; 357:266–81; Thomas K.M., Lloyd-Jones D.H., Thadhani R.I., Shaw A.C., Deraska D.J., Kitch B.T., et al., "Hypovitaminosis D in medical inpatients," *New England Journal of Medicine*, 1998; 338:777–83

24 Li Q., *Effets des forêts et des bains de forêt (shinrin-yoku) sur la santé humaine: une revue de la littérature* [Effect of forest bathing (shinrin-yoku) on human health: A review of the literature], *Sante Publique*, May 2019; S1(HS):135-143. French. doi: 10.3917/spub.190.0135. PMID: 31210473

CHAPTER 9

Brain Builders

Let's do a quick thought exercise ...

Imagine that you're standing in front of a fallen tree that you need to chop into firewood. Unfortunately, the only tool at your disposal — the only tool you've ever known — is a bread knife. It's small and flimsy but you're determined, so you start sliding the blade back and forth across the wood. It's a wildly inefficient process, it uses far more energy than it should, and it takes forever to see any progress. You can't help but sigh. *If only there was a better way!*

Now imagine that you're standing in front of that same fallen tree and someone hands you a power saw for the first time. You pull the trigger, press the whirring blades against the trunk, and are genuinely shocked — who knew that it could be this quick and easy to chop wood? Who knew there was a method that was so much more efficient? And how the heck have you gone your entire life not knowing that tools this powerful even existed?!

At this point, you might be wondering if all this talk of wood chopping is really relevant in a chapter called "Brain Builders," and the answer is *heck yes*!

Because here's the thing: most people go their whole lives desperately wanting to get more done, unlock their potential, and do good — scratch that, do *great* — work. But because they don't know how to optimize their brains, it's as if they're trying to reach their goals using a bread knife instead of a power saw.

But what if you could upgrade your flimsy knife for a tool with real grunt? What if there were simple steps you could take that would give you increased sharpness, efficiency, and horsepower? Excuse the pun, but it would be a no-brainer, right?!

Well, in this chapter we're going to show you precisely that: **how to build a better brain** — one that functions optimally, is highly resilient, is massively creative, and that makes connections and identifies patterns that others don't.

In short, we're going to walk you through the steps that will allow you to optimize the most sophisticated, powerful, and precious tool you own — the one that sits between your ears — so that you can multiply your results by two, four, even ten times.

Happily, the process is not just achievable, but far simpler than you may expect. If you're implementing the health hacks you just learned in Chapter 8, you're already part of the way there: they'll all do wonders for your brain as well as your body, especially hacks #1 (Food as Fuel), #3 (Move Your Body) and #6 (Optimize Your Sleep). On top of that, there are four more brain builders that we want to share with you, all backed by science. The first one is something that we're particularly passionate about.

Time Magic Brain Builder 1: Meditation

Meditation is the practice of observing your thoughts, training your awareness, and cultivating stillness. It's the experience of you beyond your thoughts. And get this: it can help you become a master of time.

We're not just saying that to sound "woo-woo"; it's actual science. A 2013 study from the Universities of Kent and Witten/Herdecke found that mindfulness meditation influenced how people perceived the duration of time, effectively slowing down their experience of time. So even if you make no other changes at all from this book other than starting a meditation practice, you'll *feel* like you have more time.

Meditation is also fantastic for your brain. For example, did you know that doctors in certain hospitals across the US prescribe meditation instead of drugs like antidepressants and blood pressure medication?! Yep, it's a legitimate, proven treatment for these issues.[1] Meditation has also been shown (among many other things) to reduce stress, improve attention and concentration, enhance communication between nerve fibers, and increase the levels of myelin sheathing around neurons.[2]

If you've never meditated before, or if you've tried and the habit never stuck, it might seem daunting. You might even have visions of monks on mountaintops twisting themselves into pretzel-shapes and not talking for years on end. But we promise: this practice can be so much easier, simpler, and more rewarding than you ever realized. (And no mountaintops, pretzel-twisting, or vows of silence are necessary!)

TIME MAGIC TRICK: A SIMPLE BUT POWERFUL MEDITATION TECHNIQUE

Meditation can take many forms, but here's a really simple way to get started:

1. Find somewhere quiet to sit, where you're comfortable, your back is supported, and you won't be disturbed. Cross-legged against a wall might work for you, or perhaps in a supportive chair.

2. Close your eyes. Notice your breath as it flows into and out of your body, observe what's happening.

3. With each exhalation, gently say the Sanskrit word "Om" inside your head. This is your "mantra"; a "toy" for your monkey mind to focus on.

4. As you concentrate on your mantra, thoughts may arise in your mind. When you notice that you've been caught up in a thought, gently unhook from it, let it go, and return to your mantra. Do this every time a thought comes along: *unhook, let go, and return; unhook, let go, and return*. The goal is not to hold on to the mantra, but to let go and experience yourself beyond your thoughts.

5. After ten, 20, or 30 minutes, gently open your eyes. Wiggle your toes and fingers, and feel the sensations in your body. Give yourself a few moments to sit and enjoy the stillness and inner peace you've just cultivated, then get up and go on with your day.

To enhance your practice:

- Be sure to switch your phone on silent.
- Try "1-to-2" breathing: Simply breathe in for three or six counts, and out for four or eight. The longer exhalation slides

your body into a parasympathetic state, aka relaxation mode. (This is a particularly great hack if you're feeling stressed out. It can completely change your state in just a few minutes!)

- You might like to use a meditation timer to time your practice. We like Insight Timer, which you can download for free from the app store. Determine how long you'd like your session to be, set the timer, then begin your practice. One Giant Mind is another great option.

- To really dive deep and master meditation, you can't go past in-person tuition from a trained teacher. We've studied transcendental meditation/Vedic meditation with gifted teachers, and the leaps we made in our practice during those times were significant and swift.

TIME MAGIC MASTER: DR. MARK HYMAN

Our friend Dr. Hyman MD is a practicing family physician and an internationally recognized leader, speaker, educator, and advocate in the field of Functional Medicine.

When we asked him what his #1 Time Magic Trick was, here's what he said:

"Something I do before I make a major decision, head into a busy day, or even before a workout or a stressful phone call is a breathing exercise called Take 5. I breathe in for five seconds, hold for five seconds, and breathe out for five seconds, and I do this, you guessed it, five times.

"So often we make decisions in a reactionary state before we've calmed our nervous system down. Taking time to breathe will completely change your outlook and make your days smoother."

One of the most common objections people have to starting a meditation practice is, "But I don't have time!" The fact that meditation actually slows down your perception of time flips this excuse on its head. In fact, the "busier" you are, the more you need meditation! It is precisely because time is so short that we should all be devoting some of our precious minutes to practicing meditation and becoming a master of time.

We practice Vedic meditation, a type of mantra-based meditation. We practice for 20 minutes, every day — ideally, twice a day. If we miss a session, we feel off. To some people, 40 minutes a day might sound like a lot to devote to one practice. But as one of our teachers told us, you have 72 x 20-minute time slots each day. If you take just two of those 20-minute slots to meditate, you still have 70 slots leftover, but those 70 will be more productive, peaceful, and happy because you have taken just two of them to meditate. In our books, that's excellent ROI on those small investments of time.

Of course, that's just what works for us. Forty minutes a day might not be for you. The most important thing is to start somewhere — even if that means two minutes of stillness once a day. Ideally, aim to extend your practice by a minute each week, until you're sitting for 10–20 minutes. We promise you'll notice an incredible difference in how you feel each day, even with just a few minutes of meditation.

Time Magic Brain Builder 2: Get Serious About Stress Management

None of us needs a medical study to tell us that too much stress is bad for us. (Although rest assured: there are plenty!)[3] Because let's face it: we've all felt the negative impacts firsthand — whether it's a racing mind, tight chest, sweaty palms, sleepless nights, shallow breathing, unsettled gut, inability to concentrate, raging irritability ... The list of symptoms is both long and unpleasant.

When it comes to the real estate between your ears, the news gets even worse: **chronic stress literally shrinks your brain.** A study published in the journal *Neurology* showed that the brain suffers when the primary stress hormone, cortisol, rises too high in the body's system, resulting in smaller brain volume — or, in layman's terms, brain shrinkage.[4]

Regardless of this hugely worrying study, you've likely heard the recommendation to "lower your stress levels" before. But have you ever got serious about it? Has it ever clicked for you just how important it is to shrink your out-of-control stress cycle before it shrinks the most important organ in your body?!

There are so many things you can do to reduce stress, including:

+ Meditate (see previous section)
+ Get enough movement and exercise (see Time Magic Health Hack 3)
+ Start stretching and foam rolling (see Time Magic Health Hacks 4 and 5)
+ Spend time in nature (see Time Magic Health Hack 8)
+ Get more and better-quality sleep (see Time Magic Health Hack 6).

... But we're betting that you already know all the things you "should" be doing to reduce stress.

So instead, we want to give you something far more useful and powerful: a method to embed stress-reducing activities into your daily life as a priority, so that they *actually get done*. (Revolutionary, we know!)

TIME MAGIC TRICK: SIMPLE STRESS SAVERS

(aka The tiny two-minute habits that will finally free you from stress)

Grab your journal and write out your answers to the following questions.

1.   Why is managing your stress levels important to you?
Is it the fact that your brain is in danger of shrinking? Is it that too much stress makes it hard for you to be the kind of partner/parent/friend you want to be? Is it just that it makes you feel like rubbish when your stress gets out of control? Tap into the reasons why stress management is important to *you*.

2.   What's the cost of *not* solving your stress cycle?
If stress is already impacting your life in a negative way, that effect is only going to be amplified if it's left unchecked for years.

So tell us: what's the cost of not solving your stress cycle? Is it the disintegration of your marriage? The complete collapse of your health? Is it wasting decades of your life feeling "on edge" and anxious? Is it lying on your deathbed and regretting the kind of parent/friend/sibling/partner you were?

3.   Now list 10–20 activities that meet all three of the following criteria:
a. They reduce your stress and make you feel good
b. They are easy for you to do regularly
c. They can be done in 30 minutes or less — and ideally, you want to stack your list with options that are at the one–five minute end of the spectrum.

These activities will be your go-to "Simple Stress Savers."

Make sure you follow the criteria carefully. Your ultimate stress-reducing activity might be sailing, but if you can only get out on the water once every month, that's not good enough for this list. Similarly if you LOVE playing golf, but it takes you five hours to play a single game, again: that's great, but you'll need to think of something else for this activity.

If you're *really* struggling for ideas, consider the following options as inspiration: dancing to your favorite song, repeating an affirmation, taking a bath, sipping a cup of tea in the sun, moving your body, gardening, making love, free-writing a poem or journal entry, playing with your pet, reading a book, giving yourself a dry body brush or massage, or two minutes of deep breathing or "legs up the wall" pose.

Now, here's the magic bit:
With your answers to questions 1 and 2 at the forefront of your mind, pull out your calendar (and everything you learned in Chapter 3 on Priority Planning) and start scheduling in some of these activities regularly over the next month.

At first, it might feel a bit silly to go to the effort of scheduling an activity that only takes a few minutes, but as you know, **for new habits: if it's not scheduled, it's not happening**. And soon enough, if you keep at it, these habits will become second nature and will shift into a natural, organic part of your daily routine that you won't even need to think about.

Other things to keep in mind:

- The more regularly you can schedule these beneficial activities, the more likely they are to become a habit.
- Choosing things you *like* doing means you'll be more likely to do them.

- Stacking your stress-reducing activities on top of another habit will make them more likely to "stick." For example, you might decide that every time you brush your teeth, you'll immediately follow up with two minutes of "legs up the wall" pose. This is hugely effective because brushing your teeth is (hopefully!) something that you already do without much thought or effort, so you can leverage that ease and momentum to build this new habit.

Far too often, people wait until they have a crisis before taking action on their stress levels. But by the time you're in an ambulance after having a heart attack, or you're sitting in the divorce lawyer's waiting room, it might be too late. Far better to embed these two- to 30-minute activities into your life now so that you never reach a crisis point in the first place.

Time Magic Brain Builder 3: Carefully Curate Your Content Consumption

Think of all the information you consume each day: chatter on the radio, posts on social media, the books you read, the podcasts you listen to, the news on the waiting room TV … Do you have any idea how much information you consume?

Science has the answer, and like most of the stats in this book, it will probably make your gut squirm. A 2009 report published by the University of California found that the average adult consumes 34 gigabytes of content and 100,000 words of information every single day.[5] To put that in perspective, this book is only around

70,000 words long. So you're encountering well over this entire book's worth of info *every single day*.

Here's another important question for you: how **discerning** are you about the information you consume? Are you a "Content Connoisseur," carefully curating the stuff you allow into your headspace? Or (excuse our French) are you more of an "Info-tart?"

Most people would never dream of eating doughnuts and fries five times a day, yet they have no hesitation putting junk into their brain five — or 105,000 — times a day. Not only is this nonstop consumption eating up your time, it's also cluttering up your mind and causing you to walk around with a brain that's distracted and overstuffed.

The solution? Simple: stop throwing away your precious brain space on mindless content consumption. Yes, there's a level of consumption that's healthy, inspiring, and entertaining. But the average person goes *way* beyond this level. No one seems to be talking about this, but we're not afraid to stick our necks out and speak the truth: it's time for a radical new approach to content consumption …

TIME MAGIC TRICK: BECOME A CONTENT CONNOISSEUR

This is a concept we invented to protect your precious brain from an endless stream of clutter and stimulation. Becoming a Content Connoisseur is about preserving your mental bandwidth by being highly discerning about the information you consume, no matter what the form.

We're not saying you need to abstain from content entirely, or that everything you consume needs to be "highbrow." (Sometimes an episode of *Suits* at the end of a long week can be the most enjoyable, therapeutic way to spend a Friday night!) Instead, we're simply advocating that you become *conscious* about what crosses your eyes and ears.

Here's how to change your habits and become a Content Connoisseur:

- **Become aware of the content you consume in any form.** It's easy to not even *notice* that there's music blasting at the cafe where you're working, or that you're mindlessly staring at the billboard while you're out walking the dog. Heck, there are even TV screens playing content on the side of the fuel pumps when you're filling your car up with gas! Awareness is the first and most important step, so pay attention to the content you're consuming — whether unwittingly or not.

- **Take steps to minimize mindless consumption.** You only want to consume information when you *choose* to consume it, not by default. So, for example, if you've been listening to the radio while driving, make sure you always switch it off before you turn the car off. That way, you're not bombarded with noise the next time you turn on the ignition. If you *choose* to switch the radio on, that's fine. But you want the choice to be conscious.

- **Identify your Content Black Holes.** You know when you decide to "quickly" check your social media app, only to lose yourself for a whole hour? Or when you decide to watch "just one" episode of a TV show, only to find yourself a few hours later in a full-blown TV coma? Take a moment to figure out when you're most likely to slide down that slippery slope: what time of day is it? What location are you usually in? Are there any key triggers you can identify? Then create workarounds to ensure you don't get sucked in again.

- **Never consume two streams of content at once.** Watching TV? Great. Own your choice, enjoy your time, and remain present. Do *not* pick up your phone and start scrolling through your social media feed at the same time. This is just adding clutter on top of clutter and it's not healthy for your brain. Instead of doing two things half-assedly, pick which one you want to do and focus your attention there.

Time Magic Brain Builder 4: Connect to Protect

Even though it might feel like fun and games when you're hanging out with your mates, it turns out that it's actually serious nourishment for your neural networks. Because the science is in, and it's clear: **strong social connections are crucial for brain health.**

Research shows that people who spend most of their time alone are more likely to experience cognitive decline than people with robust relationships and social ties. In one particularly shocking example, a massive study conducted over ten years that followed 12,000 participants found that when people are lonely, their risk of dementia increases by up to 40 percent![6]

So avoiding loneliness by building strong social connections may well be one of the best protective mechanisms we have for a strong, healthy brain — both now and in the future.

In Chapter 12, we're going to show you in detail how to spend more time with your loved ones and prioritize those all-important connections. For now, just know that hanging out with people you love doesn't just *feel* great, it's great for you.

TIME MAGIC TRICK: HEALTHIER HORMONES THROUGH HUGS!

Research shows that when people hug their partners or spouses, it triggers a cascade of oxytocin (the hormone of love and bonding), lowers cortisol (the stress hormone), reduces noradrenaline (one of the "fight or flight" hormones), and also lowers blood pressure.[7]

From cuddles to content consumption, we've covered a lot of ground in this chapter! With these four powerful techniques in your Time Magic toolkit, you've now got everything you need to turn your brain into the power tool it was born to be … And trust us, you're going to love the difference these neural upgrades make!

Now, it's time to take a sidestep into another topic entirely. In the next chapter, it's all about the money, honey.

Notes

1   www.wsj.com/articles/SB10001424127887324345804578424863782
    143682

2   Tang Y.Y., Hölzel B.K. and Posner M.I., "The neuroscience of
    mindfulness meditation," *Nature Reviews Neuroscience*, April 2015;
    16(4):213–25. doi: 10.1038/nrn3916. Epub 2015 Mar 18. PMID:
    25783612

3   Yaribeygi H., Panahi Y., Sahraei H., Johnston T.P. and Sahebkar
    A., "The impact of stress on body function: A review," *EXCLI
    Journal*, July 2017; 16:1057–1072. doi: 10.17179/excli2017-480. PMID:
    28900385; PMCID: PMC5579396; Kagias K., Nehammer C. and
    Pocock R., "Neuronal responses to physiological stress," *Frontiers
    in Genetics*, October 2012; 3:222. doi: 10.3389/fgene.2012.00222.
    PMID: 23112806; PMCID: PMC3481051; Botha E., Gwin T. and
    Purpora C. "The effectiveness of mindfulness based programs in
    reducing stress experienced by nurses in adult hospital settings: a
    systematic review of quantitative evidence," *JBI Database of Systematic*

Reviews and Implementation Reports, 2015 October 2015; 13(10):21–9. doi: 10.11124/ jbisrir-2015-2380. PMID: 26571279; Stavrou S., Nicolaides N.C., Critselis E., Darviri C., Charmandari E., Chrousos G.P., "Paediatric stress: from neuroendocrinology to contemporary disorders," *European Journal of Clinical Investigation*, March 2017; 47(3):262-269. doi: 10.1111/ eci.12724. Epub 2017 February 3. PMID: 28074555.; Echoufo-Tcheugui J.B., Conner S.C., Himali J.J., Maillard P., DeCarli C.S., Beiser A.S., Vasan R.S. and Seshadri S., "Circulating cortisol and cognitive and structural brain measures, The Framingham Heart Study," *Neurology*, November 2018, 91 (21) e1961-e1970; DOI: 10.1212/WNL.0000000000006549

4   Echouffo-Tcheugui J.B., Conner S.C., Himali J.J., Maillard P., DeCarli C.S., Beiser A.S. et al., "Circulating cortisol and cognitive and structural brain measures, The Framingham Heart Study," Neurology, November 2018, 91 (21) e1961-e1970; DOI: 10.1212/ WNL.0000000000006549

5   www.nytimes.com/2009/12/10/technology/10data.html

6   Sutin A.R., Stephan Y., Luchetti M. and Terracciano A., "Loneliness and Risk of Dementia," *The Journals of Gerontology: Series B*, Volume 75, Issue 7, September 2020, pp 1414–1422, doi.org/10.1093/geronb/ gby112

7   Ditzen B. et al., "Effects of different kinds of couple interaction on cortisol and heart rate responses to stress in women," *Psychoneuroendocrinology* 32, 2007, 565–574; Light K.C., Grewen K.M. and Amico J.A., "More frequent partner hugs and higher oxytocin levels are linked to lower blood pressure and heart rate in premenopausal women," *Biological Psychology*, 69, 5–21, 2005; Grewen K.M., Girdler S.S., Amico J. and Light K.C., "Effects of partner support on resting oxytocin, cortisol, norepinephrine, and blood pressure before and after warm partner contact," *Psychosomatic Medicine*, 67, 531–538, 2005.

CHAPTER 10

Wealth Wizardry

Until just a few centuries ago, humans exchanged a significant amount of their time for food. Just think: your Paleolithic ancestors had to devote many hours to hunting down a herd of gazelles or scouring the undergrowth for edible tubers and mushrooms before they ever got to sit down and enjoy a meal.

Compare that to today, when you can order any cuisine you like with the push of a button and it will arrive at your door in a matter of minutes.

A lot has changed since the caveman era, but make no mistake: we're still exchanging time to get that food. It's just that these days, instead of a direct swap, we exchange our time for *money*, and then exchange that money for food. In fact, exchanging our time for money is something that we spend more of our lives doing than any other single activity outside of sleeping.

As we saw in that handy chart in Chapter 1, the typical person spends 13.2 years exchanging time for money, which equates to 158 months, or 688 weeks, or 115,632 hours. Whatever unit you choose, it's a full 16.7 percent of the average life — a significant chunk. So in this chapter, we want to talk about money. Because in reality, money *is* time. We like the way famed investor Joel Greenblatt put it:

> *While to many "time is money," it's probably more universal to say that "money is time." After all, time is the currency of everyone's life. When it's spent, the game is over. One of the great benefits of having money is the ability to pursue those great accomplishments that require the gifts of being and time.*

So in this chapter, we're going to lead you through a powerful primer on Wealth Wizardry — aka The Time Magic Tricks that will help you have more money without having to sacrifice more time to get it.

One more thing: we are not financial planners or experts. You should consult with an independent, non–industry-funded financial advisor before making any changes to your finances.

With that out of the way, let's begin …

Step 1. Know Your Numbers

When it comes to finance, far too many people take the "ostrich approach" — they bury their heads in the sand and hope for the best. Unfortunately, this is not an effective strategy for anything in life, and especially not for managing your money. So the first step on the path to Wealth Wizardry is to "know your numbers."

There are five numbers you should know:

1. **Your monthly income**: i.e., how much you earn each month.
2. **Your necessary monthly expenses**: This is the money you spend each month on rent or mortgage repayments, bills,

groceries, etc. To determine this amount, you can either go through your bank statements or use a payment-tracking app to keep track for you.

3. **Your debts**: This is all the money you owe on things like credit cards, mortgage, car loan, student loan, etc.

4. **Your net worth**: This is a tally of all your assets (such as home, car, investments, and savings) less all your debts. (It's okay if this number is a negative: that's where most people start out, so don't worry if that's you, too.)

5. **The amount in your superannuation/401(k)/pension account**: aka your retirement fund.

The truth is, you can't make any meaningful changes to your finances if you don't know the current lay of the land. So if you don't know these amounts, it's time to pull your head out of the sand and go find out.

As you continue your journey to Wealth Wizardry, you can keep on tracking these five numbers as a way to gauge your financial health and progress.

MELISSA

I used to be a *big* ostrich when it came to my finances: it all felt "too hard," so I simply ignored them. Meeting Nick, who's always been a whiz with money, was a big learning curve for me and my attitude towards money has changed significantly since then.

These days, I'm proud to say I know all my "numbers." One of the things that Nick and I do each month to stay on top of them is to have a **Time Magic Monthly Money Meeting**.

This is a meeting we schedule in our calendars — usually for the last Friday of every month — where we go over these five numbers, plus the finances for our businesses, and any other money matters that may have come up.

We view this **Time Magic Monthly Money Meeting** in the same way that we see our regular workouts or our visits to the chiropractor — as a necessary, nonnegotiable way to take care of our health (in this instance, our financial health). It's also a great way to see where we're at with our money goals.

Sometimes, if we've got a lot going on in the business that month, these meetings might take 40 minutes, but usually they're a super quick 15–20 minutes and we've both grown to love and value them.

Step 2. Plug Your Jugs

Imagine trying to carry water in a jug that's full of holes.

No matter how hard you tried, you'd be losing water with every step. Unfortunately, far too many people go through life with their money in (metaphorical) leaky jugs, which means that no matter how much they earn, they're always hemorrhaging money along the way.

One of the quickest, simplest ways to accelerate your journey to Wealth Wizardry is to plug your jugs so that you stop losing money through those pesky little holes. Here are some holes to look out for:

HOLE 1: UNNECESSARY SUBSCRIPTIONS

"Subscription creep" is real. It seems *everything* these days has been turned into a subscription — from food delivery to ride-sharing to entertainment and more. So if you've found the number of subscriptions you have is slowly but surely creeping up, you're not alone.

Unfortunately, subscription creep is also a silent wealth killer. In a 2021 US survey, 71 percent of respondents estimated they spent more than $US50 per month on unwanted subscription fees.[1] In Australian dollars, that's around $75 per month, which equates to $900 per year, which is a lot of money to throw down the drain. But the real kicker comes when you consider the potential income you could earn on that amount if you invested it in a high interest bank account — at 3.7 percent interest over 20 years, that measly $75/month adds up to $26,136, with a whopping $8061 coming from interest alone!

One of the lowest hanging fruits then, is to go through your subscriptions and cancel any you don't love and use. For example:

+ Look at your TV/streaming services — how many platforms do you really need? Can you keep one for now, then once you've watched your favorite shows, cancel it, and try another one? *You* are in control here, not the media companies, so take the reins.
+ Same with your music streaming services — how many do you need?
+ If you're a business owner, look carefully at the subscriptions you have and be ruthless — what's serving you and what's just a leak?
+ What paid apps have you signed up for on your phone and then forgotten about?

We recommend sitting down with your bank statements and going through them, line by line, identifying the subscriptions you don't need, then cancelling them right there and then. It might take you an hour or two to do, but that hour could help you reclaim $26,136 of income! (That's a pretty good ROI, by anyone's standards!)

HOLE 2: BANK FEES

Shift to a no-fee bank account. With so many banks offering this service, it's a no-brainer — otherwise, that monthly fee is just money (and potential interest earned) that you're flushing down the toilet.

HOLE 3: YOUR PLANS AND PROVIDERS

As a customer, you have the power to spend your dollars where you want them. Just because you've "always been" with the same phone company or energy company does not mean that you have to stay there. With a little time and energy, you can potentially save hundreds, even thousands, of dollars annually by getting a better deal on expenses like:

+ Insurance (car, health, home, etc.)
+ Phone and internet
+ Energy and electricity
+ Any other regular bills you have.

Choose one of your bills, and do a quick online search. Can you find another company that offers the same service for a lesser price? If so, your first step is to jump on the phone and ring your current provider. Here's what to say:

Hi there. I've been a customer with you since [date that you joined]. I spend [dollar amount] with your company per [month/year/etc.]. I've just discovered that [insert name of competitor company here] can provide the same service for [their price]. I'd much rather stay with you than switch to [competitor company] — can I please speak to someone about adjusting my bill to match their price?

If they're not willing to lower your fee, then call the new company and make the switch. Then choose another bill and repeat the process.

For a small investment of time now, you can turn those potential hundreds saved each year to thousands — if not tens of thousands — over the coming decades.

HOLE 4: LATE FEES

Ever forget to pay a bill, then kick yourself when you get charged a late fee? Never fall prey to this annoying money-leak again by setting up direct debits for all bills where this is possible. The money will then be automatically taken from your account each billing period and you'll never be late again.

For larger bills that recur regularly (like, say, your car registration), set an automated recurring reminder in your task management app for 14 days before the bill is due, so that it's on your radar and you've got time to transfer money into the right account before the due date.

Step 3. Karate Chop Your Debts

Have you ever seen a karate master chop through a plank of wood — or even a *pile* of planks — with nothing but their bare hand? It's a sight to behold. A true master uses a seemingly miniscule amount of movement — no wind-up, no big swing, just an inch or two of mind-blowing power — to punch through the wood. From the outside, it looks like it shouldn't work. But because the master has channeled all their energy into that one tiny movement, they can generate an explosive amount of power and smash the wood into smithereens.

In this next step, we're going to show you how to smash through your debts in the same way a karate master smashes through wood — by focusing a significant portion of your financial energy on them, you're going to crush them in a way that you might not have believed possible.

Now, not all debts are created equal — there are plenty of different kinds of debts, and everyone's circumstances are different. So keep that in mind as you walk through this process and adjust the steps as needed for your unique situation.

TIME MAGIC TRICK: HOW TO KARATE CHOP THROUGH YOUR DEBTS LIKE A TRUE NINJA WARRIOR

1. Pull up the list of your debts that you created in Step 1. Make sure it includes *every* debt you have: mortgage, car loan, student loan, credit card debt, even interest free loans from your family or friends.

2. Don't freak out if you've got a lot of debt. We know that it can feel scary to see them all laid out in front of you, but take a deep breath. Know that you're taking a monumentally important step on the way to achieving Wealth Wizardry. Just start where you are *right now*.

3. Determine what the interest rate is for each of your debts, and rank them from highest to lowest.

4. Now it's time for you to choose which debt to pay off first:

   a. Some people like to start with the debt that has the **highest interest rate**. By starting here, you'll be minimizing the amount of interest you owe over the long term, which makes this a very smart choice.

b. Some people like to start by tackling the **smallest debt** or debts, to give them the feeling of a "quick win" and to build momentum. This can be hugely motivating, which also makes it a smart choice.

5. Once you've chosen which debt to pay down first, you're going to focus on it with the same intensity and energy as those karate masters. And you'll be pleased to know that by making consistent payments, even if they don't seem huge, you can pay those debts down faster than you may have realized was possible. (We'll show you where the money comes from to do that in the next step.)

6. As soon as each debt is paid off, either shutdown the loan facility or *cut up your credit card* and never get one ever again. (No, we're not being metaphorical here. We want you to grab a pair of scissors and literally slice that debt-creating, time-sucking beast of a credit card into tiny little pieces so that it can never hold you — or your time — hostage again.)

Step 4. Get Savvy About Saving

In steps 1 and 2, you minimized the money you dole *out* each month. Now let's maximize the money you've brought *in*. This step is also going to give you the cashola to karate chop your debts. It all starts with saving ...

TIME MAGIC TRICK: A SHIFT IN MINDSET

If you see someone driving around in a luxury car, you might think to yourself: "Wow, that person must be wealthy!"

But in reality, that car represents money that the person *no longer has*. The car is a signifier of spending, not necessarily of wealth. (And the two don't always go hand in hand!)

Truly wealthy people know that it's not about the money you earn that makes you wealthy, nor is it about the money you spend … It's about the money you *keep*. And by "keep," we mean save. So let's get savvy about saving.

Hopefully by now, you've sourced a no-interest bank account. Now we want you to open three of them. These three accounts are going to make managing your money and automating your savings a total no-brainer.

Once you've opened your three accounts, label them as follows:

1. **Everyday Abundance**: This is where you'll manage your everyday expenses and transactions.
2. **Karate Chop**: This is where you'll funnel the money to pay down (or "karate chop") your debts.
3. **Magic and Memories**: This is your account for fun stuff; the stuff that brings magic to your life or that helps you make memories that will last forever (think vacations and epic experiences).

When your monthly income comes in, you're going to allocate a percentage of it to each account. These percentages will change based on where you are in your journey to Wealth Wizardry.

To start with, you're going to allocate your monthly income to the above accounts like this:

60 percent: Everyday Abundance

30 percent: Karate Chop

10 percent: Magic and Memories

Let's look at each of these accounts in more detail:

YOUR EVERYDAY ABUNDANCE ACCOUNT: 60 PERCENT

This account is for nonnegotiable expenses, like food, rent, mortgage, internet, phone, and transport.

Let's do some magic here:

1. Take your after-tax income and times it by 0.6 to get 60 percent. This is the amount that should go into your Everyday Abundance account each month.

2. In Step 1, you determined your monthly necessary expenses. These are the expenses that will come out of this account.

3. Now compare the two numbers you've just found: 60 percent of your after-tax income and your monthly expenses:

   a. If your monthly expenses are less than or equal to 60 percent of your income, you're on the right track for creating Wealth Wizardry.

b. If your monthly expenses exceed 60 percent of your income, this means you're spending more than you're earning, which is a recipe for debt disaster. It also means it's time to get serious about creating change.

If your expenses are only a bit higher than 60 percent of your income, circle back to Step 2 and see what other "leaky holes" you can plug to bring your monthly expenses down even further.

If your expenses are significantly higher than 60 percent of your income, it's time to make some big cuts to your big expenses. For example: have you got a mortgage that's sending you above your 60 percent that you can only *juuuust* afford? It's time to refinance to a better interest rate that brings you below the 60 percent, or else sell and move somewhere you can actually afford. We know this is not an easy thing to hear, but we also don't want you to be a slave to debt forever.

PS: We've mentioned it already, but now would be a *fantastic* time to seek out an independent financial advisor to get expert advice and help you rewrite your financial future.

YOUR KARATE CHOP ACCOUNT: 30 PERCENT

You are going to use the money in this account to karate chop your debts into smithereens.

Essentially, this is not *your* money; it has already been allocated to your highest priority and it's going to jump you out of debt.

Choose a schedule to pay off your debts that feels good for you, whether it's weekly or monthly, and enjoy it every time you press that "pay" button.

Then, each time you karate chop another debt, do something extra nice for yourself — you deserve it, ninja!

YOUR MAGIC AND MEMORIES ACCOUNT: 10 PERCENT

This money is the cream on top for you to do whatever you wish with. Take your other half out on a date. Save up for a holiday. Buy that *thing* you've been lusting over for months. *You do you.* You've earned it.

TIME MAGIC TRICK: IF POSSIBLE, PUT YOUR TRANSFERS ON AUTOPILOT

If you get paid a regular salary, you can set up automations within your bank account so that as soon as you're paid, the different percentages of money get funneled into the different accounts.

If your income is irregular or you're self-employed, it's simply a matter of determining a schedule that works for you and then manually transferring the correct amounts into the different accounts.

Step 5. Rewrite Your Financial Future

Once you've paid off all your "bad debts" (for most people this means: once you've paid off all your credit cards and high-interest loans), we're going to shift your allocations so that you're not just karate-chopping debts, you're building wealth too.

Here's how to do it:

1. Open up two more no-fee accounts, and label them as follows:

    a. **Breathing Room** — This is the account that ensures you never have to panic when something unexpected happens. Put simply, with this clever little stash of cash, you'll always have room to breathe.

b. **Future Freedom** — This is the account that will help you create financial freedom in the future.

2. As soon as you've paid off all your high-interest debts, we're going to reduce the amount going into your Karate Chop account and redirect it to your Breathing Room account, like this:

   60 percent: Everyday Abundance

   20 percent: Karate Chop

   10 percent: Magic and Memories

   10 percent: Breathing Room

   The aim is to get *one whole month's* worth of expenses into your Breathing Room account, in case of emergency.

You already know how much one month's worth of expenses is. (This is the exact amount that you put into your Everyday Abundance account each month — equating to 60 percent of your income.) Now, it's a simple matter of funneling 10 percent of your income into your Breathing Room account for as long as it takes for you to build up that one month buffer.

As soon as you've hit that amount, give yourself an enormous pat on the back, and then for the love of all that is holy, **do not touch the Breathing Room account unless it's an emergency!**

The amount of peace and mind you'll have, knowing that this money is there for you should you need it is huge. Enjoy that feeling of safety and spaciousness!

And now, it's time for even more magic ...

3. With your high-interest debts smashed, and your breathing room now secured, it's time to look to the future. We're going to adjust your monthly allocations one final time:

60 percent: Everyday Abundance

20 percent: Karate Chop

10 percent: Magic and Memories

10 percent: Future Freedom

(Your Breathing Room account is now set aside for emergency use only.)

The money in your Future Freedom account is for you to invest. This is where you start to make your money work *for* you, building up over time and creating financial freedom for your future.

Taking money that was going to other people (i.e., paying off your debts) and now using it to build up your own wealth is *incredibly* powerful. And the best part here is that you still get to chip away — in pretty solid 20 percent chunks, mind you — at any other debts you still have *and* start to grow your wealth at the same time. #winning

As you start to pay off more and more of your debts, the amount you can allocate to your Future Freedom account will grow, until one day you'll be debt-free and your allocation will look like this:

60 percent: Everyday Abundance

10 percent: Magic and Memories

30 percent: Future Freedom

(Your Breathing Room account is still set aside for emergency use only.)

4. As for *where* you should invest the money from your Future Freedom account, that's up to you — and again, you should seek the expert advice of an independent financial advisor.

… And there you have it, friend! A simple, foolproof system for taking control of your finances, creating Wealth Wizardry and making the most of all that money you've earned in exchange for your time.

On that note, we want to take another look at that time you're exchanging for money, but from a different perspective. Because it's not just what you *earn* during those 13.2 years that matters, it's also what you're *doing* with that time ...

Note

1   media.chase.com/news/survey-from-chase-reveals

CHAPTER 11

The Greatest Magic Trick of All

We've all heard the quote, "Do something you love and you'll never work a day in your life." But how many of us actually *follow* this advice? A quick survey of your friends, family, and colleagues will likely reveal the same answer that we've arrived at: not many.

Ask people about their work and more often than not you'll be met by a chorus of answers that range from "Meh" to "My goodness, I'd rather poke myself in the eyeball than face another week of it."

This phenomenon isn't just anecdotal; the data backs it up. A global poll conducted by Gallup found that 85 percent of people are unengaged and unhappy at work.[1] This is a shocking — and heartbreaking — statistic. Especially because, as you well know, **how we spend our days is how we spend our lives**. And when you consider that the average person will spend 4,818 days — or 115,632 hours — at work over the course of their lifetime, that means there's an awful lot of people who aren't just unengaged and unhappy at work, they're unengaged and unhappy in their lives.

With so much of your life on the table, figuring out how to take your work from being an activity you either dislike or don't care about, and turning it into an activity you like, or maybe even love, is the greatest magic trick you can perform. It means you can change the entire flavor of those 115,632 hours from something that fills you with dread to something that lights you up. (Forget about pulling a rabbit out of a hat, this is so huge it's like pulling an elephant out of a teacup!)

Unpacking Our Hidden Beliefs About Work

Conversations about work can often be met with resistance. It's an area of our lives where we've all received huge amounts of conditioning — not just through 12 years of schooling, but through almost every movie, book, and fairytale we've ever consumed. The message is clear and unwavering: go to school, get a job, then work there until you retire.

Most of this conditioning rarely, if ever, gets questioned. In fact, many of us are still unwittingly carrying around beliefs left over from our grandparents' and great-grandparents' eras, or even from the early industrial revolution. Here are some outdated beliefs that we see regularly:

+ **"I should pick one career and stick with it."** Um, no. Just because your parents might have stayed in one career for their entire lives doesn't mean you have to.

+ **"Loyalty to my employer matters more than my own health and happiness."** Again, a big no! Just because your grandfather was loyal to the same company his entire life doesn't mean you need to be, or even that that's a worthy goal to aim for. Loyalty in the workplace is important, but it needs to be earned — on both sides — and should never come at the expense of your mental or physical health.

+ **"Changing careers is scary and not worth it."** We get it: changing career paths can feel daunting, especially when you add to the mix the fear of the unknown, fear of starting over, and not wanting to feel like you've wasted time in your current career. These concerns keep many people chained to the path they chose — or randomly fell into — as teenagers, even though it might be eroding their soul and sanity today. But ask yourself, what's scarier: some short-term discomfort now to make a change, or 115,632 hours spent being unhappy?

+ **"A job is the only way to earn money."** You'd be surprised how many people believe this, even though it's patently untrue. Starting and running your own business is one popular alternative (one that we love and chose for ourselves). But the possible ways to earn money are as numerous as stars in the sky. Some people even opt out of the system entirely — moving somewhere remote, growing and farming everything they need, and selling the extras for additional income as required.

The point of identifying these faulty beliefs isn't to say that jobs are "bad," or that you should quit, or that you need to run away to a remote woodland and start herding alpacas. It's simply to highlight that you — like all of us — probably have a fair few beliefs about the nature of work that you may never have even noticed, and some of them may not be serving you.

Radical Change vs. Realism

Too much advice about being happier at work falls into the dangerous territory of "rainbows and cupcakes." "Follow your bliss," blog posts will say, without offering guidance, or recognizing that you have bills to pay and kids to support. "Do what you're passionate about," they'll admonish, without acknowledging the huge amount of privilege that comes with being able to do that.

And on that note, it would be remiss of us to not recognize our own privilege in this discussion. We both do work we love, and have done for decades. An enormous amount of effort has gone into achieving this goal, and we've also been the benefactors of huge privilege. The fact that we were both born able-bodied into loving families in a peaceful and prosperous country, went to good schools and had roofs over our heads, means that we were batting above average from the get-go. We know privilege exists, we acknowledge it in ourselves, and it's an important factor to keep in mind throughout this conversation.

But let's get back to you, and helping you experience more happiness and engagement with your work. We've got plenty of strategies to share that can help, which we've divided into two categories.

1. **Small steps**: These are easy-to-execute tweaks and techniques that will help you experience more happiness in the work you're *currently doing*.

2. **Big shifts**: These are the powerful strategies that will help you shift gears entirely, break free from work you don't enjoy, and do something that actually, *finally* fulfills you.

This balance of realism and radical change will allow you to tailor a strategy that suits whatever your current situation may be. And because we're talking about such a significant chunk of your life, keep in mind that even the smallest of tweaks will snowball into massive changes over time. So let's dive in.

Small Steps to Move Towards Work You Love

These steps are for you if you have a job that you want to be happier in. If that's you, try the following.

IMPLEMENT EVERYTHING IN THIS BOOK

From Priority Planning (Chapter 3), to the Tick or Flick™ system (Chapter 4), to Ignition Intervals (Chapter 5), to mastering your phone (Chapter 6), you now have the tools and techniques that will help you quit wasting time at work and get your deliverables completed faster.

When you combine that with everything else you've read in Part 3 of this book — in particular, the Health Hacks (Chapter 8) and the Brain Builders (Chapter 9) — you've got everything you need to optimize your performance and function at your peak.

Put all this together, and you can either spend less time at work and have more time to yourself, or else impress your boss by running circles around your peers. Or you can knock everyone's socks off — including your own — by doing both.

PRACTICE "QUIET QUITTING"

Quiet quitting is when you quietly, without announcement, quit doing everything except the precise role, hours, and deliverables that you're employed for.

This means no more unpaid overtime. No more answering emails on weekends. No more taking the stress of your job home with you and letting it poison your personal time. You do your work, then you leave it behind.

If you're used to a culture of "work is life," where burnout is a badge of honor and you're expected to sacrifice your sanity, then Quiet Quitting can seem revolutionary. In reality though, it's simply a redrawing of the boundaries around what's important to you, which you have every right to do.

If you're worried that you won't get enough done if you Quiet Quit, or that your boss will be annoyed or disappointed if you refuse to stay late, we have two counter arguments for you:

1. Remember that the average knowledge worker spends a full 47 percent of their workday in a state of semi-distraction,[2] which means nearly half their working hours are spent doing slow, substandard work. It's *those* people your boss should be worried about, not you.

2. If your workplace insists on unpaid overtime, and demands that you let work encroach on your personal life, it might be a sign that more significant change is needed.

NEGOTIATE FACTORS THAT WILL INCREASE YOUR HAPPINESS

Here's a secret that plenty of employees don't realize: you can negotiate *anything*. You can bring any factor to the table that you wish and attempt to negotiate improvements. That doesn't mean your employer will go for them, of course, but it's certainly worth trying.

Factors that may improve your happiness that you might consider negotiating include:

+ **More money.** This is an obvious one, but it's worth stating anyway! (And we're going to show you how to stack the odds in your favor when negotiating for a pay rise.)

+ **More time off.** Do you frequently work unpaid overtime? Consider negotiating "time off in lieu" for those unpaid hours you've worked.

+ **More flexibility in your schedule.** Say you're a passionate surfer, and nothing makes you happier than going for a long surf each morning. Only problem is, you're supposed to be at your desk by nine, which makes it hard for you to hang ten. Why not ask your boss if you could shift your work window so that you start (and finish) an hour later every day? Or even just one or two days a week? Remember, even small shifts can make a big impact on your happiness.

+ **More location independence.** If working from home is possible, would make you happy and would save you from commuting, bring it to the negotiating table. Maybe you could work from home all the time and just come in for meetings? Or maybe you could work from home one or two days per week?

+ **More projects that you love.** Is there an area of your work that you'd like to learn more about? Are you craving more of a challenge? Negotiate these issues with your boss. Maybe there's room in the budget to send you on a training course. Or maybe you can offload a project that's not making the most of your skills, while picking up an exciting new project instead.

With all your negotiations, be creative and flexible with your suggestions, and come armed with reasons why your proposals are a win-win for both you and the company. Keep in mind that whatever outcome you achieve, you have every right to revisit the topic in the months and years ahead.

And if you don't get what you want in this round of negotiations, don't despair. Because next time round, you're going to have an edge.

GIVE YOURSELF AN EDGE

A lot of people do a half-assed job at work. So anyone who's *not* slacking off is already ahead of the game. And as for those select few who bother to optimize their work performance and give their bosses exactly what they want? Well, those people are freaking rock stars!

If you want to become the rock star of your workplace (and give yourself an edge the next time you're negotiating) follow these steps:

1. **Practice Time Magic at work.** You'll automatically jump ahead of half your colleagues if you do nothing else other than stop looking at your phone at work. Add in everything else you've learned and you're headed straight to hall-of-fame territory.

2. **Step into your boss's sneakers.** Get a copy of your job description and a list of all your projects and deliverables. Put yourself in your boss's shoes, look closely at everything you do from their perspective, and ask yourself these three questions:

   a. How can I help my boss achieve their goals?

   b. How can I make my boss's life easier?

   c. How can I make my boss look good?

   Come up with three concrete things you could do over the next 6–12 months that would achieve one or all of these outcomes.

3. **Tell your boss.** Arrange a meeting, and communicate your new goals with your boss. Ask for their feedback. Suggest a quarterly meeting to review your progress.

4. **Now go "Time Magic" the heck out of those goals.** Priority Planning, Ticking and Flicking, and Ignition Intervals are going to be your new best friends.

5. **Be a ninja at your quarterly check-ins.** Come armed with a list of the deliverables you've ticked off and the metrics you've helped improve. Ask for feedback, and accept it gracefully. Share your new or adjusted goals with your boss. And for the love of all that is holy, don't talk about your salary in these meetings. This is your chance to show your boss that you're a team player, not a ruthless climber.

6. **At your next annual performance review, present your case.** You've now got concrete evidence of your value to the company. Which means you've got a real edge when it comes to negotiating what you want. Congratulations, you're a genuine rock star — and your company is going to have to play ball to keep you!

USE THIS POWERFUL QUESTION AS A COMPASS

Ask yourself the same question that Steve Jobs reportedly asked himself every day: "If today were the last day of my life, would I want to do what I am about to do today?"[3]

If the answer is "no" for too long, it's a sign that maybe small steps aren't enough. Maybe it's time for some big shifts.

Big Shifts to Move Towards Work You Love

When small steps aren't cutting it, and you want to make major moves in your work, try the following strategies:

THINK OUTSIDE THE BOX (OR BETTER YET, CREATE YOUR OWN BOX)

Sure, you can apply for a different or better job.

But you could also step out of the job framework entirely: Start consulting. Start a business. Go freelance. Go rogue. Forget all the "rules" you've been told about what work means, and start thinking from scratch: What do you actually want? What kind of work have you always dreamed of doing? What kind of work would increase your happiness by 5, 10, or 50 percent?

BE CREATIVE

There's never been a moment in history with more flexibility in terms of how to make money and add value to people's lives. If you'd told our grandparent's generation that there would be people making money by: filming themselves putting make-up on, turning trash into artwork, reviewing roller coasters, showing people how to forage for food, composing personalized songs, or sharing their favorite product recommendations, they wouldn't have believed you. (In fact, they probably wouldn't have even understood you!) The only limit to what work you could do is your imagination.

FAST-TRACK YOUR TRAINING

If you're starting something new and need to get skilled up, there are more options than ever before to help you gain expertise fast.

MELISSA

When I first started my own business more than a decade ago, I felt *way* out of my league. I truly knew nothing about how to run a business.

On hearing this, a well-meaning relative suggested that maybe I should go to university and study business — a three-year, $30,000 commitment.

While that might be a great option for some people, I knew that I only needed a few solid skills in a really specific area — online business — in order to start earning and growing.

So instead of the old-school route, I opted for an eight-week online course that cost a fraction of that amount, but that still taught all the skills I needed to get started.

That single course gave me an incredible foundation from which to grow my fledgling business, which has since become a global operation with multiple streams of income and an audience of millions.

I'm so grateful that I followed my own intuition in that moment, and didn't waste three years of my life buried in a classroom learning stuff I didn't need.

We're not dissing formal education here, far from it. There are some careers where it's an absolute necessity. What we *are* saying is to look for creative ways to learn the skills you need, and to be mindful to not use extended study as an excuse to not get your tush in the arena and start trying.

BABY STEPS ARE COOL

Our friend Sarah desperately wanted to leave her corporate gig and become a creative writer. To make the journey easier and less scary, she started with a series of "baby steps," each one inching her closer to where she wanted to be. At first, she set up shop writing resumes — it wasn't her dream business, but it was certainly better than her corporate role, and she was at least developing skills that would get her closer to her ideal job.

Within three months, she'd added websites and blog posts to the list of writing services she provided. Within 18 months, she was also writing books and magazine articles — the exact sort of creative writing she'd always longed to do, but that had felt out of reach at first. By taking baby steps, Sarah ended up exactly where she always wanted to be.

FOLLOW YOUR CURIOSITY

Sometimes the advice to "do what you love" or "do what you're passionate about" can feel overwhelming, especially if you don't know what your passion is.

If that's the case for you, it's time to ask yourself some different questions:

+ What are your strengths?
+ What would people pay $100 to hear you talk about?
+ What do other people tell you you're good at?
+ What are you curious about?
+ What did you love doing as a kid?
+ What problem do you see other people have that you always wish you could help them with?

By lowering the bar from "what you're passionate about" to "what you're curious about," you can take the pressure off, give yourself some breathing room, and allow yourself to start exploring all the possibilities that lie in front of you.

IT'S NEVER TOO LATE TO MAKE A CHANGE

With all that conditioning we receive about work and career paths, it's easy to think that it's "too late" to make a switch. We vehemently disagree. It's *never* too late to make a change — especially when it's your health and happiness on the line.

If you're worried that it's "too late" for you, begin gathering evidence of people who've started new jobs, businesses and career paths later in life. We'll kick off the list for you: J.K. Rowling was 36 when she had her first book published. Vera Wang didn't start designing clothes until she was 40. Julia Child published her first cookbook at 50. The beloved folk artist Anna Mary Robertson Moses (aka Grandma Moses) didn't begin her painting career until age 78. And author Harry Bernstein wrote countless manuscripts that were all rejected until finally having his first "big hit" at the grand old age of 96.

The takeaway here, put simply, is that it is never *ever* too late to make that change. And on that note …

Friend, Your Elephant is Waiting

We told you at the start of this chapter that we'd help you perform one of the greatest magic tricks of all time: to transform your work from something that you don't enjoy, to something that you like or even love — aka pulling an elephant out of a teacup.

You've now got the strategies to do exactly that, and your elephant is waiting.

If you're feeling a bit (or a lot) of fear about making these changes, we want to say two things to you:

Firstly, when we say that small changes add up to big results, we mean it. If you negotiate just *one day* of working from home each week, you'll save 103,680 minutes over the course of your working life — that's more than ten whole weeks of your life that you'll be reclaiming, from one tiny, measly change.[4]

Now imagine compounding those changes — say you start working from home two days per week, you quit doing unpaid overtime, and you get a 10 percent raise after your rock star performance. Over the course of your working life, those three small changes, when compounded, add up to you reclaiming over *two whole years* of your life and adding $414,133 to your personal income. Talk about small changes with elephant-sized results![5,6]

Secondly, we've said it before and we'll say it again: your time is precious. Your happiness matters. And there's so many things you can do to create change. So with all these powerful tools and strategies right here in front of you, the question ceases being "How can I stop being so unhappy at work?" and becomes something else entirely …

"What the heck am I waiting for?"

Notes

1   news.gallup.com/opinion/chairman/212045/world-broken-workplace.aspx?g_source=position1&g_medium=related&g_campaign=tiles

2   Killingsworth M.A., Gilbert D.T., "A wandering mind is an unhappy mind," *Science*, November 2010; 330(6006):932. doi: 10.1126/science.1192439. PMID: 21071660

3   thoughtcatalog.com/brianna-wiest/2015/11/12-daily-routines-of-famous-people-in-history-and-what-you-should-take-from-each/

4   Want to see how we got these figures? The average Australian commutes for 48 minutes per day. Forty-eight minutes x 48 working-weeks of the year = 2304 minutes saved per year. Over a 45-year career (working from age 20–65), that equates to 45 x 2304 =

103,680 minutes = 10.29 weeks saved, when you work from home just one day per week.

5   Want to see how we got these figures?

Work from home two days per week: Per above note, this saves 103,680 minutes for one day per week over a career, for two days per week that's 103,680 x 2 = 207,360 minutes = 4.73 months saved.

Quit doing unpaid overtime: The average Australian does 319 hours of unpaid overtime per year = 319 hours/year x 45-year career

= 14,355 hours = 19.66 months saved.

So total time saved = 4.73 months (commute) + 19.66 months (unpaid overtime) = 24.39 months = just over two full years saved total.

For income: The average Aussie earns $1769.80/week (source: www.abs.gov.au/statistics/labour/earnings-and-working- conditions/ average-weekly-earnings-australia/may-2022). A salary raise of 10 percent = $1769.8 x 10 percent = an extra $176.98/week.

Over 52 work-weeks (assuming the employee receives holiday pay), that equals: $176.98 x 52 = $9202 extra income per year.

Over a 45-year career, that one single raise equals: $9202 x 45 = $414,133

If you continue your rock star performance at work, repeatedly proving how valuable you are to your employer, you can get many raises over the years. So this single strategy can equate to *millions* of extra dollars in your bank account over the course of a career.

6   Way back in the Introduction, we said it was possible to reclaim 16 years of your life using the techniques found in this book (an estimate that we believe is conservative). Using the two techniques you just learned in the preceding paragraphs (working from home two days per week and opting out of unpaid overtime at work) it's possible to reclaim two years; with the game-changing phone hacks in Chapter 6 (Digital Drain), it's possible to reclaim 11 years; and by implementing the techniques described in Chapter 7 (Email Emancipation) you can add another 3.5 years to that tally. So in just three of the chapters of this book, there's a massive 16.5 years back on the table. #winning

If one — or even all — of these particular techniques aren't options for you, think back to Principle 8 of the Time Magic Mindset Step 8: Look for reasons why (not why not). Which of the many other tips and strategies in this book could you implement instead? How could you get creative to find an alternative that works for you?

Whatever path you choose, in Part 4, we're going to show you some excellent things to do with all that newfound time you've just reclaimed.

PART FOUR
Reaping the Rewards

You've now saved time, you've optimized every part of your day, and you're well on your way to creating the spacious, fulfilling existence you've always dreamed of. The next question to answer is this: **what could you do with all your extra time?** In this next section of the book, you'll learn how to transform your time off, how to find hobbies that you love (even if you have no idea what lights you up), why resting isn't "lazy" but essential, how to find meaning in your life (without running away to a monastery), and the science-backed answer to the question "What makes life worth living?"

CHAPTER 12

Transform Your
Time Off

*"What we do during our working hours determines what we have;
what we do in our leisure hours determines what we are."*

GEORGE EASTMAN

In 1930, the average person worked 50 hours per week. That might sound like a lot, but it was actually down from 65 hours per week a mere 30 years earlier — those 1930s peeps had it good in comparison!

It was in that year, in that context, that famed British economist John Maynard Keynes wrote and published an essay that contained a startling prediction that shocked both experts and the public: Keynes thought that by the time his grandkids came of age in the late twentieth century, **the average person would be working just 15 hours per week**. In fact, he predicted that the biggest problem that would plague humankind in today's world would be **what to do with all our time off.**

Turns out Keynes was a *little* off with his prediction. Scratch that, he was way off. On average, a full-time employee in the United States today works 37.5 hours per week[1] (which equates to 1801 hours per year, and 11.92 total years of work over a lifetime) — more than double the 15-hour work-week he foretold.

But even though Keynes missed the mark with the first half of his prediction, he was bang on the money with the second half: most people still have no idea what to do with their time off.

It's probably why, when we do have free time, so many of us reach for whatever seems easiest at that moment — which usually means scrolling our phones, binge watching TV, mainlining snacks on the couch or otherwise numbing out with food, alcohol, drugs, online shopping, gambling, or porn — because we simply don't know what else we should do.

Of course, even though those activities might be "leisure" in the sense that they're "not work," often they're not even that enjoyable — they're just a mindless habit that our brains have fallen into to fill a void. They're certainly not nourishing for your body, mind, or soul. In fact, some of those activities can be downright harmful for your physical health, mental health, and relationships.

So that's why, in this chapter, we want to give you a roadmap to **transform your time off**. We're going to show exactly how to "magic" your time off into something that you get excited about, that fulfills you, transports you, engages you, nourishes you, and enriches all other aspects of your life. Heads up: this might just be the most fun and rewarding chapter of the whole book. So strap yourself in, leave your preconceptions behind, and get ready to enjoy the ride.

The Point of Extra Time (and Where Most People Get It Wrong)

As you know by now, the point of reclaiming your time (and making more of it) isn't to just keep stuffing your calendar and to-do list with more responsibilities, or to spend those extra hours at your desk or computer.

The *actual* point is to infuse all your time — including those weeks, months, and years you've just alchemized out of nowhere — with love, meaning and fulfillment. That's why Time Magic is so radically different from traditional approaches to time management. (And it's why this book can help you get such radically different results.)

And the first method we're going to look at to bring in more of that love, meaning, and fulfilment is to do … nothing.

Rest: The Life-Changing Magic of Doing Absolutely Nothing

In some ways, it's wild that so many of us struggle to do nothing. After all, what could be more natural than resting? As kids, we did it so effortlessly. And now here we are as grown-ups, having to "work" at rest.

On the other hand, it's not surprising at all! We've talked already about the deep, destructive conditioning that's led so many of us to intrinsically link our self-worth with our productivity and how much we get done. And it's easy to see the flawed logic our brains buy into:

1. "My worth depends on how much I get done."
2. "Rest is doing nothing."
3. "Therefore when I rest, I am worth nothing."

Melissa has battled with a version of this thinking pattern, with some pretty toxic consequences.

MELISSA

For the past ten+ years of my working life, I've been someone who gets a lot done — to the point where friends and family would openly marvel at my output! In hindsight, I can see that a part of my identity became wound up in how much I achieved and how much I got done. I got a huge sense of satisfaction at the end of a workday when I could look down at my computer and see that I'd written 2000 words of a book, or that I'd mapped out a brand new online program. I'm not gonna lie, it felt good! And I started to think of myself as "someone who gets a lot done."

Still, I *did* take time off. I wasn't exactly an A+ student at resting and relaxing, but I did it semi-regularly.

That is, until I became a mama.

After our daughter was born, I knew that I wanted to take maternity leave. So for eight glorious months, I was focused wholly and deeply on my little one. (Let me pause for a moment to say that yes, I am extremely privileged to be in this position, and yes, there are so many systemic changes that need to be made to our laws, workplaces, and culture at large to make it possible for more mothers and parents to spend this precious time with their babies.)

During that time, it was like I gave myself a "free pass" to not work. I let go of my to-do list and business goals and felt zero guilt about it. I simply reveled in the experience of motherhood.

Then, at around the eight-month mark, something shifted. A small part of me started putting her hand up, as if to signal, "Hey, I wouldn't mind stepping back into that part of my life again." So I started dabbling in my business again, while my daughter was napping.

But once I'd started back at work, it was like the floodgates opened and that old feeling of getting satisfaction from getting things done kicked back in. And without me realizing it, my self-worth once again started being fed by how much I'd achieved.

The problem was, I had less time than ever to do *work*-work, with so much of my time beautifully filled up with motherhood.

My solution — illogical and flawed though it was — was to throw myself into work in any spare moment I could find. Which basically meant that every minute that wasn't devoted to our little girl was suddenly spent going full-tilt at my work. And doing anything besides those two activities — mothering or working — felt like a complete waste of my time.

So yep, you guessed it: rest was off the cards.

For the first time in a very long while, I felt guilty for resting. I'd feel "lazy" whenever I did it. Even on those days where I was exhausted, I still drove myself to "get more done."

Eventually, the complete lack of rest and the relentless pushing caught up with me, and I entered a state of burnout. If you've ever experienced burnout, you'll know that it's a highly unpleasant experience.

For me, it felt like a combo of stress, exhaustion and overwhelm that I couldn't shake. I'd get teary over random things, I didn't cope with stuff that ordinarily wouldn't have bothered me, and I always felt like I was on the verge of a meltdown … So, you know, loads of fun for everyone!

It took a while, but slowly I started recalibrating my priorities, resetting my own expectations, and giving myself permission to rest.

But the very first step I took — and where you might want to start too — was becoming aware of and examining the very real beliefs and conditioning I'd picked up about rest, worthiness and everything else that's tied up in those topics.

Tell us, what do you believe about rest?

If your ideas about rest are not as healthy and constructive as you'd like, you're certainly not alone. Our western culture has been heavily influenced by the **"Protestant work ethic"** — a sociological concept that attaches supreme value to hard work, and that (in its strictest sense) literally views hard work as the route to eternal salvation.

Even though the term refers to the Protestant religion, in reality, it applies to everyone (even if you're not religious) because it's pretty much baked into the fabric of our society. In fact, it's hard to overstate the influence this concept has had on our shared cultural values, and it's even harder to escape the long tendrils of its conditioning.

For example:

+ Maybe you grew up watching your mother or father work themselves to the bone to provide for the family, barely ever taking time off and living in a state of perpetual exhaustion.
+ Maybe you spent time in a school environment, sporting club, friendship group, or other culture that valued hard work, forward movement, and progress over everything else.

+ Maybe you absorbed a message from the people around you and/ or the media that you have to "earn" your rest; that it can only be indulged in after you've hit some nebulous threshold that says you've "done enough."

+ Maybe you were raised to think that you work hard until retirement age, and that resting before then is "lazy."

Understanding what underlying beliefs you have is a powerful first step to rewriting them. So let's dig in.

INSPO-ACTION: YOUR REAL THOUGHTS AROUND REST

Ask yourself: What do I really believe about rest?

Some prompts that may help you explore this question:

• What was I taught about rest in my family of origin (whether overtly or implicitly)?

• How was rest modeled for me when I was growing up?

• What do I think when I see other people resting?

• What do I think *other people* think if they see *me* resting?

• Have I got invisible criteria in place that I must meet before I let myself rest? What are they? Where did they come from?

You might like to journal your answers to these questions, or spend some time in solitude or out in nature pondering them.

If you've got some work to do in the area of rest, there's good news: you can rewrite your conditioning and become the type of person who embraces and embodies rest.

Here's how:

INSPO-ACTION: THE BIG REST REWRITE

Now that you know what your current beliefs are around rest, you can begin reframing them.

Get out your journal and explore the following questions:

- What do you *want* to believe about rest?
- What does deep, restorative rest *feel* like to you?
- Think of a child in your life whom you love and care for — what do you want them to believe about rest, who is worthy of it, and when they are "allowed" to do it?
- Speak to yourself as a child. Think back to when you were five, ten, 15: what do you wish you could say to Young You at a time when you were feeling tired, exhausted, and depleted?
- Think back to a more recent time in your life where you pushed yourself really hard. What do you wish you could say to Past You? What did you need during that time? What did you deny yourself? Why?
- You might even like to write a letter of apology to your Past Self, apologizing for all those times you've ignored your own need for rest. Tell yourself what you'll do differently moving forward.

Remember, there's only one person who gets to determine your beliefs around rest: **you**.

That said, if it helps spark your creativity or curiosity — and if it helps you give yourself permission to embrace the art of doing nothing — we're going to share our beliefs about rest here. But remember, these are *our* beliefs, we're not telling you what you should believe.

HERE'S OUR "RESTIFESTO" (THAT IS, OUR REST MANIFESTO!)

+ We believe that all humans (that includes you!) are worthy of rest by the pure fact that they are alive.

+ We believe that rest is an act of resistance. In a culture that preaches hustle, busy-ness, and pushing at all costs, rest is rebellion.

+ We believe that rest is an act of self-love. It is a powerful, loving way to honor oneself.

+ We believe that rest is a practice. It's not a "one and done" type of thing, it's something you have to engage in and implement regularly.

+ We believe that rest is an act of personal hygiene. In the same way that you wouldn't even *think* about starting your day without brushing your teeth, we believe no one should even think about strong-arming their way through life without incorporating regular periods of rest.

+ We believe there's no need to "earn" rest, or offset it. You are worthy of it now, with no hoops to jump through or boxes to tick.

+ We believe that different things are restful to different people, and that's okay. It's all about figuring out what feels restful and restorative to *you*.

TIME MAGIC TRICK: WRITE YOUR OWN RESTIFESTO!

Write out your new, updated beliefs about rest — the stuff you want to embody in your life, that reflects how you want to care for yourself.

Stick your Restifesto up somewhere where you'll see it, and reread it regularly.

Bonus points if you display your Restifesto somewhere other people will see it (like on your fridge), so they can be inspired by your deep commitment to honoring your innate need for rest.

Okay, so we've established why so many of us have messed up beliefs around rest, you've examined your own beliefs and rewritten them into a restifesto, and now you're all pumped up to embrace rest in your life ...

... But, um, how do you actually *do* rest?!

To some people, this question will be laughable. ("How do you rest? Duh, you just *rest*!")

But we know that for many of you reading this book — especially the Type As and the recovering people-pleasers (Hi! That's us too! Welcome to the club, we're so pleased to have you here!) — it's not quite as simple as just setting forth into the wide world and *resting*. After all, this is an activity you may have spent a lifetime avoiding, feeling guilty about, or actively trying to hide from!

So we get it, and we've got you covered. For those of you who are new to resting, here are our top four strategies for slowly and gently incorporating deep rest into your daily life:

1. **Embrace the art of the daydream.** You might have grown up thinking that daydreaming was "a waste of time" or something that only slackers did. But the science is in, and it's clear: daydreaming is not only a natural, healthy state for your brain, it's also excellent for replenishing your mental energy after times of focus, it helps with decision making, it improves performance of later tasks, and it can increase mindfulness.[2] So kick back, stare into space, and let those daydreams carry you away!

2. **Focus on your senses**. For those of us used to constant
   action, resting can feel weird. It can even make your brain
   feel "itchy
for activity. To overcome this problem, try out this sneaky
   strategy: make your brain happy by giving it something to
   focus on that's still conducive to rest. A great way to do this is
   to shower your senses with pleasurable, enjoyable stimulation.
   For example, spread your softest, comfiest blanket out in your
   backyard, strew some cushy pillows on top, put some gentle
   music on in the background, then lie down and let the sun
   and the wind caress your skin. Delightful!

3. **Take a wide-angle view of the world**. Gazing off into
   the distance, ideally at nature, is a great way to let your mind
   wander and your body relax — and it's doing your body and
   brain good at the same time. Stanford neurobiologist Andrew
   Huberman says that looking at a horizon or a broad vista
   releases a mechanism in the brain stem linked to vigilance and
   arousal. In an interview with *Scientific American*, he explained
   how engaging in this type of panoramic vision can turn off
   your stress response and induce calmness.[3] Our favorite place
   to gaze into the distance is on the cliffs overlooking our
   favorite beach. If there are no clifftops or grand vistas near you,
   kicking back and staring up at the clouds can have a similar
   effect.

4. **Sit with the discomfort of doing nothing.** If you're
   struggling with internal resistance to rest, it might be useful
   to sit with that discomfort and learn to build up tolerance
   to it. Start with a goal of just five minutes of doing nothing.
   Notice what comes up: what do you feel? What impulses
   are cropping up? What happens if you allow that resistance

to simply be there while you continue to do nothing? This is a powerful exercise, and you might be surprised what comes up!

TIME MAGIC MASTER: GABBY BERNSTEIN

Number-one *New York Times* bestselling author, speaker and podcast host Gabby Bernstein knows the power of rest.

She builds periods of rest into her work days — not just because she knows it helps her get more done, but because it's a divine act of self-care that keeps her performing at her peak.

We've always admired how Gabby honors her need for rest, so we asked her to share her best tips with us.

"One of my favorite mantras is 'I can speed up by slowing down.' Let me give you an example of how I apply this to my workday ... and get a shitload done!

"My energy starts to crash midday. I used to force myself to work through the afternoon slump to try to accomplish more. But, I actually got less done, and the work that I did in that low-energy state wasn't as high-quality as it could have been.

"Now, I have a new daily ritual. At around noon, I do a 40-minute meditation. After that, I do 30 minutes of exercise. As I walk or do Pilates on the mat, I can feel the stagnation shifting in my body. By the time I'm done with this ritual, I feel replenished and recharged.

"Now that I consciously create space in my day to protect my energy, I'm more productive than I've ever been."

TIME MAGIC MASTER: BRONNIE WARE

Bronnie Ware is an author, songwriter, and motivational speaker best known for her juggernaut book, *The Top Five Regrets of the Dying*.

We've known Bronnie for years, and couldn't resist asking for her take on this. Her approach to rest is slightly different from Gabby's, but it's no less effective; she's earmarked a regular spot in her weekly schedule to switch off and relax:

"I never make plans on Saturday mornings. Our friends know that any time after midday will work for my daughter and me. We allow our bodies to let go fully on Friday night and wake when they're ready. Then we enjoy the timelessness without pressure. This habit has come to sustain me for the whole week ahead."

Sounds amazing to us! And it's a great example of taking a Time Magic principle and making it work for your unique routine and lifestyle.

Okay, so now you're all rested up and you're looking for something else to do with all your glorious, delicious time off. What else can you fill it with? We've got a suggestion.

High-Nutrient Leisure

According to Aristotle — yep, he of the toga and ancient Greece fame — leisure was not just an enjoyable thing to include in one's life, it was the ultimate aim. It was the highest ideal that humans could aspire to; a truly noble pursuit.

But when Aristotle spoke of leisure — and when we speak of it here — he wasn't talking about passive, mindless activities one does to pass the time. (In ancient Greece, that might have meant faffing about in the courtyard with a stone tablet. In modern times, that might mean faffing around on the couch with a digital tablet!)

No, when Aristotle spoke of noble leisure, he meant activities that stretched a person to their fullest realization; that helped them become their greatest self. It's *those* activities that he was — and we are — so passionate about, and that can transform your time off into something truly magical.

So what kinds of leisure activities are we talking about?

We like to use food as an analogy here. So many activities that modern humans reach for in their time off (scrolling, shopping, TV, etc.) are the equivalent of chowing down on a big bag of Cheetos — they might be easy to scarf down in the moment, but they're not actually filling you up, they're not doing you any good, and let's face it: you're going to feel kinda gross afterwards.

Compare that to what we call "High-Nutrient Leisure" — the broccoli and brussels sprouts of the leisure world! These are the activities that require your undivided attention, that require energy and commitment, that stretch you, that better you, and that fill you up on a heart and soul level.

These are the activities that can transform your time off from "meh" to magical. And these are the activities we want you to start engaging in as much as possible.

So what are High-Nutrient Leisure activities? Well, it can be any activity that:

+ Requires your **undivided focus**. (Hint: if you can listen to a podcast or scroll social media while you're doing an activity, it's not a High-Nutrient one!)
+ Is not passive. These activities **involve effort** and even "work," in the sense that you need to work to maintain concentration, push through learning curves, and figure out how to do things.

+ Is something that you can get better at; in which you can **pursue mastery**. (Compare that with scrolling on your phone: ain't much you can master there!)
+ Can jump you into a **flow state**. (More on this shortly.)

Some examples include: playing a musical instrument, learning a language, assembling a complex wooden model, painting a canvas, big wave surfing, reading, or writing poetry or other literature, or restoring an old car engine.

With all these activities, it's the **intention** you bring to the activity that renders it High-Nutrient Leisure or not. Consider the difference between a world-class chef bringing all their energy, attention, and creativity to coming up with a new recipe, versus a home cook popping on some music and dancing round the kitchen while she concocts a new version of her favorite curry. Both options are great and nourishing; it just depends what kind of experience you're seeking. All the activities we've described here may **feel hard** while you're starting out or when you're leveling up. This means that to engage with them meaningfully, you need to tolerate being uncomfortable from time to time and to embrace new challenges.

TIME MAGIC TRICK: FIND YOUR FLOW

You may have heard of "flow states" before. This mental state was first popularized by psychologist Mihaly Csikszentmihalyi. It's when you get so absorbed in an activity that you become supremely focused, time seems to slow down or speed up, and you become one with what you're doing.

Flow states are so rewarding and fulfilling that Csikszentmihalyi said that they are the answer to the question: "What makes a life worth living?"[4]

- So a hugely effective Time Magic Trick (and one of our personal favorites) is to find an activity that helps you achieve a flow state, then intentionally engage in that activity as often as you can.

"BUT I'M TOO TIRED FOR HIGH NUTRIENT LEISURE!"

When you've just wrapped up a big workday and you're utterly exhausted, it might seem counterintuitive to then engage in an activity that requires high levels of focus and energy.

But that's the funny thing about these activities ... they actually *give* you energy.

NICK

Writing songs and practicing music are two of my favorite activities in the world — and they're the two High-Nutrient Leisure activities that can jump me into a state of flow faster than anything else.

That said, they also happen to require a ton of energy and concentration. (Case in point: I sometimes walk out of my studio covered in sweat and weak from exhaustion.)

So you wouldn't think that I'd be able to do these activities after a long day working in front of the computer, would you? But funnily enough, that's not the case.

For me, it almost feels like I've got two internal batteries — one that fuels my "work" stuff and one for my music. If

I've depleted my work battery after team meetings, product development, or reviewing marketing campaigns, I'll reach a point where I can no longer keep achieving a high-quality output on those kinds of tasks. But instead of downing tools and flopping on the couch, I find that if I completely change the picture, pull out my guitar or keyboard, and start jamming, I've suddenly got a whole new store of energy to pull from — the backup battery has kicked in!

The reverse is true, too. On days where I've put in an intense songwriting session and have exhausted all my creative juices, I can then jump into (say) a profit-and-loss report and find a new energy and flow there.

For me, it feels like the complete change of context allows one part of my body and brain to recharge while I'm using another part. This sneaky Time Magic trick also allows me to do more of the activities that matter to me and share more of my gifts with the world — it's a total win-win.

Of course, we'll be the first to admit that there are times where you actually *don't* have the energy — or the desire — for High Nutrient activities, and that is totally fine.

In those times, you need to reach for something else to fill your time off.

Spare Time Smoothies: Leisure That's Easy to Digest!

Sometimes, sitting down and eating a whole bowl of broccoli or brussels sprouts just seems too hard!

We get it. In those times, when your body, mind, and soul actually need something that's easier and lower key, it's tempting to reach for the junk food/Cheetos version of leisure — aka your phone or the other usual suspects we've been banging on about throughout this chapter.

But as a practitioner of Time Magic, you now know that those activities aren't doing you any favors and might even be actively harming you.

So you'll be pleased to know that there's a happy medium that we want to share with you, and we're going to go back to our food analogy to explain it.

Years ago, Melissa worked as a health and life coach. Back when she was still seeing clients one on one, one of the most common questions she'd get asked was about what to eat when time and energy were short. As one client said in a session: "Tell me what to eat when I'm exhausted! I need something that's nutritious, quick, easy, and super tasty, otherwise I won't eat it!"

In those instances, Melissa had one go-to answer: smoothies. Smoothies are the quickest, simplest, yummiest way to get a whole bunch of nutrients in your belly — and best of all, they're easy to make and (in the client's words) super tasty!

We want to bring the same principle to your time off. When you're not in the mood for High-Nutrient Leisure, we recommend instead reaching for a Spare-Time Smoothie — an activity that doesn't take a heap of effort or concentration, that's "easily digestible" (aka easy to do!), but that's still nourishing to your body, mind, and soul.

SPARE TIME SMOOTHIE IDEAS:
PICK AND MIX YOUR FAVORITES

- Arts and crafts
- Baking
- Caring for your pets
- Coloring in
- Dabbling with paints or crayons
- Dancing
- Decluttering
- Experimenting with a new recipe
- Foraging
- Gardening
- Hiking
- Journaling
- Knitting
- Making fermented foods
- Making soaps, candles, body lotions
- Origami
- Pressing flowers
- Propagating plants
- Reading something fun
- Researching your family tree
- Rollerblading
- Sailing
- Scrapbooking
- Skateboarding
- Snorkeling
- Stamp collecting
- Surfing
- Swimming
- Walking

Note that you can do many of these activities with music or a podcast playing in the background, or with a friend while having a fun conversation. If that's how you want to roll, great. This is about what *you* enjoy and what makes *you* feel nourished.

Ultimately, it actually doesn't matter what specific leisure activity you do in your time off; it's what you *bring* to the activity as well as what the activity does for you. We've also found that most people need both these types of leisure in their life — High-Nutrient and Spare-Time Smoothies — because they provide different types of nourishment, and we've personally noticed that we thrive best with both in our lives.

Now that we've got leisure sorted, what other things can you fill your time off with to dial up the love and fulfilment in your life?

It's time to go beyond solo activities and look to the people you love.

Meaningful Connections

It's almost so obvious as to sound silly: spend time with your loved ones and you'll feel more meaning and fulfilment in your life.

But stick with us, because even though it might be trite advice, it's also true. The science on this is robust and clear: spending time with loved ones is crucial for health and happiness — to a greater extent than most people realize. Did you know, for example, that researchers can better predict a person's levels of overall health and wellness by looking at the **strength and structure of their circle of friends**, than by looking at the health data on their Fitbit?[5] Yep, it's true. Time with loved ones can also help lower blood pressure,[6] lower stress levels,[7] enhance your psychological well-being,[8] reduce risk of death from cardiovascular disease,[9] may help encourage a healthy lifestyle,[10] and can even help you live longer.[11] (We'll be talking a lot more about that in Chapter 14.)

But you know what? We don't need studies to tell us that time with our loved ones is good for us because we already know it, and we're betting you do too. How good does it feel to belly laugh with your besties, to have a deep, juicy convo with that old friend who knows you so well, or to sit in companionable silence with your partner?

The answer? So damn good!

So if we know this already intuitively, and if the science backs it up, why can it still feel so hard to find time to spend with our loved ones?

Here's one reason: have you ever heard the term, "the squeaky wheel gets the grease?" So often our work commitments "squeak" at us (or yell at us!) if we neglect them for a day — or even a few hours. But our loved ones, because they love us so much and are presumably great people, don't "squeak" when we have to postpone a catch-up or when we can't make it to Sunday lunch. So even though they mean more to us than our deadlines or our boss, they're actually easier to ignore.

Of course, the whole "ignoring your loved ones" technique only works up to a point. Then those relationships you care about so deeply can deteriorate or even break down altogether. Like what happened with our friend Lachlan.

Lachlan was a bigwig director of a huge multinational company. He enjoyed certain aspects of his role (like the big salary), but he didn't much like the work itself and he certainly didn't like the huge amount of hours he had to work (usually around 60 hours a week) ... Lachlan had a wife and two young boys whom he loved dearly, but with all those hours spent in the office, he didn't get to see them as much as he — or they — would have liked. He rarely made it to their soccer matches, he never got to take them to swimming lessons, and he missed most weeknight mealtimes (let alone big things like school plays and assemblies). Whenever we caught up with him, he'd enthusiastically tell us and the rest of our friends about his big life plan: he was going to continue working these crazy hours until he was 50, then he'd be "set for life" and could retire, and he'd have all the time in the world to spend with his wife and kids.

But you know how this story ends, don't you? By the time he was 40, his marriage had imploded and his relationship with his kids suffered. He's now 44, single, still working round the clock to build his retirement fund, and only sees his boys every second weekend.

Now, we're not here to set unrealistic expectations and preach impossible standards. Unless you've got a magic genie or a trust fund, we all need to work to pay bills and put food in our mouths. And there are always going to be soccer games or Tuesday night dinners that get skipped for whatever reason. It's just life, and there's no need to beat yourself up about it.

That said, we know that many people wish they spent more time with their kids/parents/friends, but then struggle to take action on this wish or aren't sure how to make it a regular part of their life.

If that's you, and the distance between what you *want* to do and what you feel like you have capacity for is a gaping chasm, these four strategies can help:

1. **Eat with your loved ones**. Eating a meal together is one of the loveliest, most gratifying experiences to share with your loved ones. And from a time perspective, you're already eating, so why not make that time do double-duty and nourish your soul while you're nourishing your body?!

   If you've got kids, sharing a nightly meal together is one of the simplest ways to ensure you're creating space for conversation and deep connection. For us, it's one of the nonnegotiable rituals in our household that we truly love and value.

   If your family has a nontraditional schedule and dinner doesn't work for you, get creative: maybe your family ritual could be a communal breakfast instead? Make this idea work for you, whatever your lifestyle may be.

2. **Exercise together**. Again, this is something you're likely already doing, so why not make the most of it?

   If you're not the world's best exerciser, doing it with someone else can be the kick in the tush you need to get moving, and it can make it so much fun.

   The obvious options are to share a walk or a hike with your loved one, but you might like to do a yoga or Pilates class together, take a surf together, go for a swim together or be "barbell buddies" at the gym. One of our personal favorites is to take a dance class together — we both get our heart rates pumping while having important time together as a couple. We love it.

3. **Find your "third thing" with them**. Way before cafe culture had become commonplace, when Starbucks was first opening its doors, their objective was to become the "Third Place" for customers — a place between home and work; a third place; a special place.

   We've tweaked this idea a little. We want you to find a "third thing" with your partner or kids — a "thing" you both love to do together, that's neither theirs nor yours, but something that's shared, that's your special *thing*.

   One couple we know found a shared love of renovating old houses. Another couple we know fell in love with scuba diving. And another couple are mutually obsessed with their vegetable patch. All those "third things" are mutual interests that feel hugely enjoyable and fulfilling to them while also strengthening their relationship.

   You can take the same approach with your kids. Nick has a "third thing" with our teenage son, Leo: rock climbing. They love nothing more than heading out together and either climbing up a cliff or abseiling down one. They will happily tell you that it's one of their favorite and most fulfilling things to do in life.

4. **Play together**. We are passionate about play. In fact, playfulness is one of our core values, especially when it comes to parenting. And play is also a brilliant way to spend time with your loved ones.

With little kids, play is remarkably simple — follow their lead, get down on their level (literally: squat, sit, or even lie down), and let yourself be as goofy and silly as you want.

With bigger kids and adults, play might be more structured (card games, board games, lawn games), or it can be just as silly and goofy as with a toddler (think: pillow fights, kitchen dance-offs, even a good old tickle wrestle).

Finally, if you're struggling to prioritize time with your loved ones, or if you're finding it hard to stay present when you're with them due to the siren song of your work, your phone, or that pile of dirty laundry, stop and ask yourself this question: **When I'm 79, would I pay money to come back to this moment and enjoy it one more time?**

Big question but if the answer is yes, then do whatever you can to stay there. *Now* is your time. *Now* is your chance. It's safe to say that you will never, ever, *ever* regret spending time with the people you love, and it's one of the most powerful ways to infuse meaning into your life.

And while we're on the subject of meaningfulness, it's time to delve even deeper into this life-changing concept and unpack the steps and techniques that will help you bring even more of it to your life — not just to your time off, but to **all** your time here on this planet. We're going to do that in the next chapter.

Notes

1   clockify.me/working-hours
2   AIPC Article Library: "The Benefits of Intentional Daydreaming."
    www.aipc.net.au/articles/the-benefits-of-intentional-daydreaming/
3   www.scientificamerican.com/article/vision-and-breathing-may-be-
    the-secrets-to-surviving-2020/
4   www.ted.com/talks/mihaly_csikszentmihalyi_flow_the_secret_to_
    happiness
5   Lin S., Faust L. Robles-Granda P., Kajdanowicz T. and Chawla N.V.,
    "Social network structure is predictive of health and wellness," *PLOS
    ONE*, 2019; 14 (6): e0217264 DOI: 10.1371/ journal.pone.0217264
6   Thoits P., "Stress, coping, and social support processes: Where are we?
    What next?," *Journal of Health and Social Behavior*, 1995; 35:53–79
7   Cadzow, R.B. and Servoss T.J., "The association between perceived
    social support and health among patients at a free urban clinic," *Journal
    of the National Medical Association*, 2009, 101: 243–250
8   Thoits P., "Stress, coping, and social support processes: Where are we?
    What next?," *Journal of Health and Social Behavior*, 1995; 35:53–79
9   Brummett B.H., Barefoot J.C., Siegler I.C., Clapp-Channing
    N.E., Lytle B.L., Bosworth H.B., Williams R.B. and Mark D.B.,
    "Characteristics of socially isolated patients with coronary artery
    disease who are at elevated risk for mortality," *Psychosomatic Medicine*,
    2001; 63:267–72
10 Reblin M. and Uchino B.N., "Social and emotional support and
    its implications for health," *Current Opinion in Psychiatry*, 2008, 21:
    201–205
11 Lunstad J., Smith T.B., Layton J.B., "Social relationships and
    mortality risk: A meta-analytic review," *PLOS Medicine* 7(7), 2010;
    e1000316. doi.org/10.1371/journal.pmed.1000316

CHAPTER 13

Your Meaningful Life

What makes a life worth living?

Many people go through life thinking the answer to this question lies in money, fame, beauty, power, success, and recognition. But do these things actually give life meaning?

Olalla Oliveros was a Spanish supermodel with a flourishing career when she began grappling with this very question. With TV roles, advertisements, and print campaigns to her name, she'd achieved what so many people long for and yet so few achieve: she'd "made it" as an actor and model.

Then, just as she landed the biggest job of her career — a starring role in a big-budget film — she shocked her home country and the fashion world at large by walking away from it all to become ... a nun.

In a scene that sounds like it's straight out of a movie, Olalla was visiting the Sanctuary of Our Lady of Fátima in Portugal when she experienced a sudden spiritual calling so strong, it felt like an "internal earthquake." It came during a time of increasing dissatisfaction in her life, so she decided to heed the call. "The Lord is never wrong," she said in a 2014 interview with Spanish newspaper *El Diario de Carlos Paz*.[1] "He asked if I [would] follow him, and I could not refuse." So she walked away from the career she'd spent her life building (and that so many people would give their left kidney for), swapped high fashion for a blue nun's habit, and joined the semi-cloistered Order of St Michael.

Olalla rarely speaks publicly any more, so we can't know for sure, but looking at the bold actions she took to redirect her life, it's not a long shot to surmise that she was seeking meaning, and found it in a nunnery. So what does that mean for the rest of us?

If you've been paying attention, you'll have noticed we've been leaving breadcrumbs throughout this book about *meaning*. Whenever we've talked about all this extra time you've been saving, reclaiming, and optimizing, the message has been clear: **use this newfound time to do what's *meaningful* for you**. But what does that actually mean? And how the heck do you do it?!

If you're worried that we're about to tell you to renounce your worldly possessions, don a sackcloth robe and run off to join a religious order, you can unclench those cheeks! We're not here to do any such thing. Instead, what we *do* want to do, is unpack the nature of "meaning" itself — what it is, why it's crucial for your wellbeing, and the surprising places you can find it. We also want to drop a truth bomb on you, and reveal why a book about time is the absolute best place to have a discussion on meaning ... but let's not get ahead of ourselves. First things first: what *is* meaning?

Making Sense of Meaning

Even though the concept of "meaning" might feel nebulous and hard to pin down, there's actually an extensive body of science on the topic. The definition that we like most is that meaning is the feeling, deep in your bones, that you "matter in some larger sense. Lives may be experienced as meaningful when they are felt to have significance beyond the trivial or momentary, to have purpose, or to have a coherence that transcends chaos."[2]

In other words, meaning is when you feel connected to something bigger than yourself, and when you feel that what you're doing matters.

It might surprise you to learn that having meaningful experiences isn't just a "nice to have" item on the menu of life, it's a "need to have" one. Yep, meaning belongs in the same category as food, movement, and sleep — things you can't live without. Sure, you can go much longer without meaning than you can without food. But just as a diet of junk food will leave your body malnourished and desperate for nutrients, a life devoid of meaning will leave your soul famished and craving fulfillment. In both cases, you'll likely feel pretty rubbish.

But a meaningful life doesn't just feel good; it's good for you and has huge benefits for your health, your wellbeing, your social ties, even your finances. An extensive longitudinal study found that people who had more meaning in their lives experienced benefits as wide ranging as:

+ More income
+ Stronger relationships (both romantic and platonic)
+ Richer social lives
+ Better mental and physical health
+ Fewer symptoms of depression

+ Fewer instances of chronic disease
+ Healthier lifestyles.[3]

Living a meaningful life has also been linked to living a *long* life. In research conducted in longevity hotspots around the world (known as "Blue Zones"), one common theme observed among the centenarians studied was a strong sense of meaning or purpose in their life. (More on this in Chapter 14!)

So if meaning is so great for us, and impacts so many areas of our life, how do we get more of it?!

Surprisingly Simple Sources of Meaning

You know we're suckers for simplicity, so we've looked at the research (which identifies many potential sources of meaning), and we've condensed things down to create a "model for meaning" that's as simple as humanly possible to both understand and — crucially — to action.[4]

So here, in no particular order, are the three most common places that people find meaning:

1. **In service to the divine**. This includes the practice of spirituality, religion, and other devotional practices like prayer, meditation, and yoga. Someone who feels a strong spiritual calling (like Olalla Oliveros did) falls into this category, as does someone who finds meaning through their faith, or through studying sacred texts.

2. **In service of achievement**. This is when you get meaning through the pursuit of a big, hairy, audacious goal — often

one that's an act of contribution (for example, you might be driven to set up a school for underprivileged children) or that will leave behind a legacy (you want to be the first to climb a particular mountain, or to make an important discovery in your field).

3. **In service of connection**. This is when you experience meaning through caring, loving, intimacy, and deep emotional connection. This category includes parents who find great meaning in raising their children, or partners who find deep fulfillment in the act of loving and nurturing each other and their relationship.

Stop Should-ing on Yourself

Of course, that's not to say that these are the only ways people find meaning; these are just the most common ones. So if you find meaning in a different way, that's awesome — you do you.

In fact, that might be the most important message of all when it comes to finding meaning: *you do you*. Because here's the thing: one person's version of a meaningful life could be another person's nightmare.

Take being a parent. For us, having kids gives our life more meaning than perhaps anything else we do in our lives. But we have friends who *don't* want to be parents just as passionately as we *do* want to be parents. For those friends, having kids would not be a path to fulfillment — just because it brings meaning to *our* life doesn't mean that it will bring meaning to *theirs*. The point of all this is that you need to figure out what gives *your* life meaning, then steer your ship in that direction.

This can sometimes be tricky, as we often feel like we "should" do certain things to find meaning. Consider, for example, the person who goes to church every Sunday because they think they should, even though they stopped believing long ago. Or the societal conditioning that tells us we "should" get married and have a mortgage and babies, even if that whole notion fills you with dread. Both those choices work for some people, but not others. They bring meaning to one person, but not the next. The good news is *you* get to decide what's meaningful for you. And as challenging as it may feel, one of your most important jobs on this planet is to create **your own version of a meaningful life**, even when it means disappointing others.

"The best day of your life is the one on which you decide your life is your own. No apologies or excuses. No one to lean on, rely on, or blame. The gift is yours — it is an amazing journey — and you alone are responsible for the quality of it. This is the day your life really begins."

BOB MOAWAD

A Side Effect, Not a Quest

Funnily enough, people who put lots of effort into searching for meaning have been found to be less happy and satisfied with their lives.[5] It seems that maximum levels of fulfillment don't come from the seeking itself, but occur when meaning is a by-product of other activities.

The secret to a meaningful life, then, may lie not in a grand quest, but in the everyday choices we make: to pursue what's important to us, to engage fully, to do the right thing, to follow our curiosity, to connect deeply, and to listen to the whispers of our soul when it tells us whether we're on the right track or not.

THE SURPRISING SPIRITUAL SIDE EFFECTS OF PRACTICE: NICK

I've played a musical instrument for almost as long as I can remember — first the flute, then the saxophone, and later the piano, as well as singing.

As everyone knows, a big part of learning any instrument is practice, and luckily for me, I learned to find meaning in practice from an early age.

Whereas other kids found that daily half-hour of songs and scales to be "boring" or "tedious," I found it highly fulfilling to devote myself to the journey, to witness transformation over time, and to slowly — sometimes *painfully* slowly — develop a sense of mastery.

Though I never would have articulated it this way as a kid, in many ways, practice became a "spiritual" activity for me. Even now, when I sit down to practice playing or singing, when I'm in the zone, it feels like I'm becoming one with something bigger than myself — maybe the music, maybe the muse, who can say.

As an adult, I've transferred this skill to other areas of my life and developed a range of different practices, all of which give me meaning in different ways. My meditation practice, for example, has been a profound source of fulfillment, as has my yoga practice, and even my fitness training I see as a "practice" of sorts.

It seems there's something unique about devoting yourself to a craft again and again, which gives enormous scope for growth and fulfillment. I'm grateful every day for the meaning I find in all my practices.

Right Here, Right Now

Although we've positioned this chapter next-to-last in this book, meaning certainly shouldn't come last in your life. It needs to be embedded in the here and now, in the day-to-day.

Too often people don't prioritize the activities they find meaningful because they don't have enough time and there's always a bunch of more urgent tasks to do first … then they wonder why life doesn't feel meaningful any more.

For some people, maybe it's simply easier to focus on finite things like the housework or the monthly bookkeeping report, rather than do the sometimes painstaking soul-scraping inner work of shifting your life in a meaningful direction.

Now that you're nearly at the end of this book, you've got the time. Or at the very least, you know how to find it. That's why a book about time is the best place to talk about meaning: because you've already overcome the biggest sticking point people cite as their reason for not taking action.

With no excuses left on the table, and a world of possibility at your fingertips (and in your schedule), it's simply a matter of prioritizing what's important to you, whether those meaningful experiences are big or small, profound, or profane.

So to wrap up this chapter, we're going to share two short but powerful exercises to help you prioritize meaning in your life and figure out what it is that nourishes your soul.

INSPO-ACTION: ASK THIS FOR MEANING: MELISSA

Since becoming a mother, an overwhelming feeling that I've had repeatedly when caring for or playing with our daughter, is a deep sense of "This is what I was put on this planet to do."

It feels like an inner knowing; a homecoming; an exhalation of sorts. That feeling lets me know I'm living my own version of a meaningful life.

I also feel this way when I'm doing work I love.

So to help you steer towards your own version of a meaningful life, try asking yourself: "When do I feel like I'm doing what I was put on this planet to do? What activity gives me that feeling?"

The answer may surprise you.

INSPO-ACTION: WRITE YOUR OWN OBITUARY

When all's said and done, what do you want your life to have meant?

And what legacy do you want to leave behind?

A simple but powerful way to find the answer to these questions is to write your own obituary. To do this, cast yourself forward to the end of your life. Imagine you've just shuffled off this mortal coil and passed on.

After you're gone, what do people say about you? What gifts did you give the world over your lifetime? How are you remembered?

It's apt that we're wrapping up this chapter by touching on the end of life, because that's also where we're headed next. In the upcoming chapter, we're going to look at the incredible, science-backed ways you can push back the end of your life — that is, extend your time here on planet earth — far beyond what is currently considered "normal." Crucially, we're also going to ensure that you're not just maximizing the years of your life but also the life in your years. Curious about how it works? Skeptical if it's even possible? Don't worry, we were too. But just wait till you discover what we found out.

Notes

1   www.christiantoday.com/article/spanish.model.olalla.oliveros. quits.entertainment.industry.to.become.a.nun.the.lord.is.never. wrong/38239.htm

2   King L.A., Hicks J.A., Krull J.L. and Del Gaiso A.K., "Positive affect and the experience of meaning in life," *Journal of Personality and Social Psychology*, 90(1), 2006, 179–196. doi.org/10.1037/0022-3514.90.1.179

3   Steptoe A. and Fancourt D., "Leading a meaningful life at older ages and its relationship with social engagement, prosperity, health, biology, and time use," *PNAS Proceedings of the National Academy of Sciences of the USA*, 116(4), 2019, 1207–1212. doi.org/10.1073/pnas.1814723116

4   Personal Meaningful Profile-Brief (PMP-B) © Paul Wong, 1998, www.drpaulwong.com/wp-content/uploads/2018/03/ Personal-Meaning-Profile-Brief-PMP-B-Wong-1998-Scale pdf; Heine S.J., Proulx T. and Vohs K.D., "The meaning maintenance model: on the coherence of social motivations," *Personality and Social Psychology Review*. 2006; 10(2):88–110. doi: 10.1207/ s15327957pspr1002_1. PMID: 16768649

5   Steger M.F., Oishi S. and Kashdan T.B., "Meaning in life across the life span: Levels and correlates of meaning in life from emerging adulthood to older adulthood," *The Journal of Positive Psychology*, 2009, 4:1, 43–52, DOI: 10.1080/17439760802303127

Time Alchemy

Medieval alchemists sought — among other pursuits — to create an "elixir of immortality." This elixir would, it was believed, grant the drinker eternal life and endless youth. It would also cure all disease.

Unfortunately, with limited tools (and no peer-reviewed journals!) at their disposal, the alchemists of yore failed in their efforts. The quest lay abandoned for centuries, only to be picked up again by a most unexpected crew: scientists on the frontiers of human knowledge; a group of people whose rigorous methods are the exact opposite of those old-school sorcerers, and yet there's no doubt that they're creating magic.

These modern, evidence-based "alchemists" are doing what was believed to be impossible even just a decade or two ago: extending the human life span. Through carefully researched strategies, they are flipping the hourglass of our lives on its head, and causing the sand to run backwards. Though "eternal life" and "endless youth" may still be a way off, what they are achieving — both in labs and in practice — is still astonishing.

So in this chapter, we're going to pull back the curtains on what these peer-reviewed pioneers have discovered, reveal their methods, and explore the question, **"How can I make *more* time?"** The answers will astound you.

CHAPTER 14

Everyday Longevity

Every quest has a starting point; a moment that sends our brave protagonist on a journey into a strange new world where they're not quite sure what they'll find or if they'll come out the other side the same person.

This quest, the pursuit of Everyday Longevity, is no different.

The starting point was rather innocuous: a high school athletics meet. Who could have guessed that that one unwitting moment would send our audacious protagonist searching for secrets from lands far and wide, and on all kinds of strange and wondrous adventures — from eating algae, to naked squatting, to dunking his head in a bowl of freezing water (yes, really).

It's a surprising story — with even more surprising results. Are you ready?

NICK

I didn't know it at the time, but I grew up in a house with a father who was decades ahead of his time.

Seeing my dad meditating under one of my sibling's cots or strapping tiny EMS (Electrical Muscle Stimulation) pads on his body so that he looked like Bruce Lee was just a normal day in the Broadhurst household. And come to think of it, not much has changed in the next generation!

My own passion for health, wellness, and biohacking began as a teen. When I was 15, I rocked up at our school's annual athletics meet. Sport generally came easy to me, and I was what you'd call an "all-rounder." I used to enter into most of the events for fun and didn't take any of it too seriously. That is, until something caught my eye: a horizontal bar about the height of my head — the high jump.

A single thought ran through my mind: *I can jump over that.*

Rewind a few years before that pivotal day, and I was a 165-centimeter teeny tweeny with aspirations of being able to slam dunk a basketball by the time I was 15 — the same age that Michael Jordan was when he first did it. (Not aiming my sights too high or anything!)

Day after day, I would play for hours — first trying to touch the net that hangs below the rim, then the rim, and finally a slam dunk. I jumped and jumped and practiced and practiced. It was exhausting, but I kept going. Soon, my basketball mates started noticing my vertical transformation and gave me a nickname: "Spring." And then it happened: during a local competition, I saw an opportunity when a ball bounced off the ring. Anticipating where it would go, and buoyed by the adrenaline of competition and spectators, I leapt into the air and … slam! I did it. My hard work had paid off.

Back to that horizontal bar. Competing in the under-16s high jump comp, I quickly found myself with no one to compete against as I kept easily clearing each new height. Eventually, the teacher in charge moved me over into the "open" competition against the 18-year-olds. Soon enough, the same thing happened, and I was standing there with no one to compete against and a bar that had yet to be touched.

By this time, all the other events were finished and the entire grandstand was focused on me. Over the loudspeaker came the announcement: "Nick Broadhurst is about to attempt the state record." None the wiser, I floated over the bar to the roar of the crowd, and realized that I might just have a knack for this whole jumping thing.

Things escalated quickly from there. I was spotted by talent scouts and entered into a training squad aimed at identifying the next generation of superstars for the Sydney Olympics. My coach at the time suggested I stop consuming dairy and gluten, which I immediately felt made a difference and allowed me to train harder and faster. Maybe too hard, actually: in my first national-level competition, when attempting the national record, I fractured my left heel bone upon lift-off and had to hobble off the field and begin a grueling recovery.

My Olympic aspirations were dashed, but a lifelong interest in health had been sparked.

That said, the topic fell off my radar for close to a decade until 2009, when I was hit with a severe case of meningitis followed by a diagnosis of chronic fibromyalgia a year later. (Lucky me.) Riddled with pain all over my body, with the libido of a 90-year-old and the stamina of a senile sloth, I had little choice but to take radical action. It felt like my life hung in the balance and to a degree it did. I got super serious about all aspects of wellness, went "next level" with my biohacking, and sought out advice from the world's best doctors, experts, peak performers, and health ninjas.

Slowly but surely, it paid off. At the time of writing, I'm 43. And I can safely say that I look and move like someone who's a decade younger, I'm fitter and stronger than when I was 20, and my energy is more "supersonic" than "sloth."

As soon as my health bases were all well and truly covered and I felt back to my old self — actually, *better* than my old self — I switched my focus from recovery and healing to something that I call Everyday Longevity. I became obsessed with figuring out the best of the best: the stuff that can literally add years to your life and radically improve your health. The stuff that sounds like it's straight out of a science fiction movie … but it's actually science. The stuff that works like *whoa*.

And that's what I want to share with you here.

What Is Everyday Longevity?

Everyday Longevity is a collection of simple practices and tools that can radically extend your life span (the length of time you live) as well as extending your *health* span (that is, the length of time that you're in good health). Because let's face it: extending your life span isn't really that great if you're in pain for those extra years, or if your mental and physical health is in a state of rapid decline. We're guessing that you, like us, want to experience wonderful, glorious, outrageous good health well into your twilight years and beyond, and that's exactly the goal of everything you're about to read.

When it comes to longevity, it can be cool and sexy to talk about the latest breakthroughs in advanced technologies — like pluripotent stem cells, gene therapy, and organ regeneration. These have their place and represent the cutting edge of longevity science. But what if there were things you could start doing today that are just as — if not *more* — powerful than the more expensive fancy-pants solutions?

We believe there is, and the science backs us up. So that's what we're sharing in this chapter.

To determine what made the cut to qualify as "Everyday Longevity," we applied strict criteria. Everything in the following pages:

+ Is effective and backed *overwhelmingly* by solid science.
+ Is cheap or cost-effective to implement.
+ Is fun, incidental, or at least easy to do.
+ Decreases your chance of dying prematurely.
+ Extends your health span, not just your life span — because who cares how many candles there are on your birthday cake if you don't have the VO_2 max to blow them out! (Ahhhh, nerd humor. Seriously though, your cardiovascular health is crucial and we'll get to it shortly.)

Some of the recommendations that follow may seem simple, but that's the whole point. The simple things in life are easy to do, which means they are also easy *not* to do. If you are serious about giving yourself the best chance at enjoying a long and healthy life full of vitality and free of disease, then buckle up — we're about to take a wild ride to the frontiers of science.

Let's start with the low-hanging fruit.

Get More Plants on Your Plate

In Chapter 8, we discussed how the food we eat matters, and that a nutritional philosophy based primarily on plants is the most scientifically validated path to great health.

This way of eating is also clearly linked to increased longevity. Studies have shown that the more vegetables eaten, the better the outcomes for breast, bowel, and kidney cancers,[1] along with a reduced risk of developing lung, throat, and esophageal cancers.[2] Meanwhile, the consumption of whole grains and pulses can have a profoundly protective effect against obesity, cancer, type 2 diabetes and cardiovascular disease.[3] In fact, studies have shown that people with the highest intake of whole grains had a 17 percent lower risk of dying from *all* causes.[4] (If that's not a good reason to cook up a big bowl of spelt pasta or a steaming pot of wild rice, we don't know what is!)

Even something as simple as eating a serving of nuts five times per week may lower your risk of developing heart disease by 40–60 percent.[5] So go ahead, grab that jar of nut butter and schmear away!

Put simply, the more plants you put on your plate — including fruit, vegetables, nuts, seeds, pulses, legumes, fungi, seaweed, herbs, and spices — the more years you'll add to your life, and the more life you'll add to your years.

All right, so now you know *what* to eat for your longevity. Next up: *how much* should you eat to prolong your life and health span?

NOT TOO MUCH

Ever felt great while you were eating a meal, then a little while later suddenly felt uncomfortably stuffed?

It's not your imagination.

When your stomach sends a signal to your brain to say that it's had enough food, the signal takes around 20 minutes to register. Unfortunately, during that time you've been blissfully unaware, so you've kept eating — only for the icky, bloated feeling to arrive 20 minutes later when the damage is already done.

Luckily, there's a super simple fix for this: stop eating when you feel like you're 80 percent full. That way, you are making sure you are not overeating beyond 100 percent.

In Okinawa, Japan — one of the world's longevity hotspots (also known as a "Blue Zone") — they have a name for this practice: *Hara hachi bu*. Scientists believe that following the principle of *hara hachi bu* and only eating until they're 80 percent full is one of the key reasons that Okinawans live so long.[6]

From a Time Magic perspective, it's such a simple tweak that can seemingly have a significant impact on your longevity, so why not give it a try today?

If you want to experience even more benefits, you may want to consider intermittent fasting (IF), the practice of partially abstaining from eating for a set amount of time. Though this practice has been a staple of many religious and cultural traditions for thousands of years, it's experiencing a renewed wave of interest in the health world right now, in particular for its profound impact on metabolism, weight loss, and cognitive function.[7]

As for its role in longevity, you know the saying, "What doesn't kill you makes you stronger?" That's exactly what is going on with IF. Done correctly, fasting causes a period of short-term acute stress (due to the temporary food deprivation) which triggers something known as *hormesis*, a compensatory defense response which sets off an array of protective mechanisms inside your body that can enhance your overall health.

It's also thought that fasting activates various signaling pathways and biochemical processes that optimize physiological function and performance, thereby slowing the progress of disease and aging.[8]

Everybody is different, and only you will know if IF is right for you. If you do want to try it, start slow, and build up.

TIME MAGIC FASTING

One of the easiest ways to reap the benefits of IF and turbocharge your weight loss is with what we call *Time Magic Fasting (TMF).*

Simply skip dinner once a week and eat smaller meals at night for the remainder of the week. For most people, this is a safe way to kickstart a powerful chain reaction in your body. (And keep in mind, dinner shouldn't be too late — always finish your meal 2–3 hours before bedtime to avoid disrupting your sleep and to allow your body to initiate its cleanup processes.)

For us, we've found that the easiest way to take advantage of this powerful longevity hack is to have our dinner early (so we're finished eating by 5:30 p.m.) and to then eat breakfast the following morning at 8:00 a.m. This provides an easy and consistent window of at least 14 hours with no food every single day.

Time Magic Fasting may not be the most *hardcore* biohacking strategy out there, but as we always say: the best strategy is the one that you will stick to! For us, TMF is it.

A few extra things to keep in mind:

- TMF is not a remedy for overindulgence. This strategy won't compensate for an overall junky diet.

- If you are pregnant or breastfeeding then you may want to wait until you try TMF.
- If you're someone with a history of disordered eating, this also might not be the hack for you.

As always, speak to a qualified holistic health practitioner before implementing anything new into your routine.

All right, so far, we've got: Eat food. Mostly plants. Not too much. What's next?

OMG, Omega-3s

Unless you've been living under a rock, you've heard the news that omega-3s are good for you. But did you realize that they can also help you live longer?

Yep, higher levels of omega-3 in the blood have been shown to increase life span by a whopping five years.[9]

Before you race off to place a bulk online order though, know this: the source of your omega-3s is important. Here's why: most omega-3 supplements (like fish oil) and foods (like salmon) are sourced from the ocean, which can damage our oceans and marine ecosystems and is *not* a viable strategy for the long-term health of our planet. Fish and fish oil have also been found to contain alarming amounts of microplastics due to destructive fishing methods and environmental pollution.[10] Every time you ingest them, you may also be ingesting those microplastics — which is the opposite of ideal!

Does this mean you shouldn't eat omega-3s? Absolutely not, especially when there's a simple solution: just cut out the middle man. Except in this scenario, the middle man is actually a middle *fish*.

See, the reason fish are so high in omega-3s is because they eat microalgae which concentrate in their flesh. So why not just go straight to the source and eat the algae itself, thereby saving a whole lotta fish, and preventing a whole heap of overfishing, bycatch, and marine destruction?! You'll also save yourself from ingesting that hefty dose of microplastics, which unfortunately have tainted almost every aspect of marine life.

Algae oil is rich in the two key components of omega-3s: EPA and DHA. So taking an algae oil supplement daily is a very powerful longevity hack for your toolkit.

It's certainly not the only solution though — walnuts, chia seeds, and flaxseeds are all great sources of alpha-linolenic acid (ALA), the plant-based omega-3 essential fatty acid that the body converts to EPA and DHA (albeit at a lesser extent to some other sources).

A recent meta-analysis found that ALA intakes between 1 and 2.5 grams per day had a protective effect against heart disease, while every 1-gram increase of ALA was linked with a 5 percent decrease in death from all causes, including cardiovascular disease.[11]

That means including just a handful of walnuts alone as a snack, or topping your oatmeal, coconut yogurt, or salads with some freshly ground chia or flax, is a powerful and easy Everyday Longevity hack. Now that's some tasty Time Magic for you!

Fiber: The Forgotten Superstar Of Health and Longevity

Some healthy hacks seem exciting and sexy. Some seem decidedly *not*. Unfortunately for fiber, it's been relegated to the unsexy end of the spectrum. Which is a shame, because this unsung nutritional hero can do mammoth things for both your health and your longevity.

A 2015 meta-analysis published in the *American Journal of Epidemiology* found that people who ate the most fiber reduced their all-cause mortality by 19 percent, compared to those who consumed the least amount of fiber.[12] It also seems likely that more is better: when researchers examined the lives and diets of 980,000 participants, they found that for every 10 grams of fiber they ate, their mortality risk was slashed by 10 percent. The effect was cumulative, so 20 grams of fiber equated to a 20 percent drop in mortality risk and so on. That's huge!

If you're about to run to the kitchen to grab some fiber right now, hold tight: this is not fiber like your grandma taught you. So if you're thinking of old-school fiber options — like a bowl full of processed bran cereal, or a spoonful of artificially flavored fiber supplement stirred into a glass of OJ — think again.

The best way to reap the benefits of fiber is to eat a diet that's high in plants, and that's also high in plant *diversity*. Basically, you want to eat a lot of plants, and mix it up. Studies have shown that people who eat 30-plus different types of plant-based foods each week have a far more diverse gut microbiome compared to those who ate fewer than ten plant foods per week.[13]

A good rule of thumb is to aim for 30 "plant points" each week. That's 30 different types of plants per week from fruit, vegetables, wholegrains, legumes (including beans and other pulses), nuts and seeds, herbs, and spices. You get one point per serving and a quarter of a point for each serving of herbs and spices. Easy-peasy.

So how will you get your 30 plant points this week?

LET'S TALK ABOUT POOP

You could probably tell (smell?!) this topic was coming from a mile away. Because let's face it: no discussion of fiber is complete without a quick mention of how it exits your body: hopefully in nice, smooth bowel movements that are as good for your health as they are satisfying for your soul!

Studies have shown that there's an inverse association between the frequency of bowel movements and cardiovascular mortality[14] — in other words, the more often you poop, the less likely you are to die of cardiovascular disease.

The good news is that with a fiber-rich diet, you can expect more magical movements to start happening naturally. So aim to eat enough fiber that you're "going" multiple times per day. Also, your movements should be well formed. We call them "smiley logs" — regular "smiles" in the bowl is your new longevity goal!

How Much Fiber Do You Need?

The average adult eating a standard western diet gets around 15 grams of fiber per day. The current dietary recommendations suggest 25–30 grams of fiber per day.[15] But we'd like to go out on a limb and say that those numbers are nowhere enough for optimum health and longevity.

For guidance on how much fiber to eat for optimized wellbeing, we prefer to look to a different source, a much older one. And prepare yourself, because we need to talk about poo again. This time though, it's actually *fossilized* poo we need to discuss.

"Paleo poo," as it's affectionately known, is fossilized fecal matter that is dug up during archaeological excavations then studied by scientists. This dried-up dung actually has a surprising amount to teach us, especially about fiber, because what scientists have now found over and over again is that this Paleo poo, no matter where in the world it's dug up, is jam-packed with one key nutrient: fiber. And a lot of it.

After taking a look at the standard amounts of fiber that modern humans are eating, do you want to guess how much fiber there was in the average caveman's diet, based on how much they were excreting in their poop? Prepare yourself: it's a giant 104 grams each day.[16] That's 3–4 times the recommended daily intake, and a walloping 4–5 times what most people are getting!

Proponents of the "ancestral" philosophy of eating point out that if our ancestors — who arguably subsisted on a diet made up entirely of the foods our bodies were evolutionarily designed to eat — were pooping out 104 grams of turdtastic fiber each day, then that's a better number for us modern *Homo sapiens* to aim for than the measly "official" recommendations.

That said, 104 grams of fiber a day is a lot. (Nick tried to hit it one day by eating as many high-fiber plants as he could, but he only made it to 94 grams! What a bummer.)

Still, we like to set our sights high when it comes to fiber and we recommend you do too.

Your Mum Was Right

It turns out that when your mum told you to eat your broccoli, she was right! And not just for the fiber.

It has long been known that consuming green vegetables was related to a reduction in the risk of developing certain types of cancer.[17] But there is one superstar molecule called sulforaphane that has only started receiving attention recently but that has already been shown to play a crucial role in aging and neurodegeneration.[18]

It may have a complicated name, but it's very easy (and cheap) to get healthy doses of sulforaphane into your diet. This compound is found abundantly in everyday vegetables from the cruciferous family such as broccoli, cauliflower, kale, brussels sprouts, cabbage, bok choy, watercress, and rocket (also known as arugula). Cooking cruciferous vegetables can significantly reduce the formation of sulforaphane,[19] but this can be avoided by simply sprinkling some yellow mustard seed powder on your veg (just a tiny amount will do the trick), which provides an enzyme that counteracts the effect of cooking (so much so that it's practically like eating them raw).

If you really want to take your sulforaphane game to the next level, you can't go past broccoli sprouts — aka the sprouted seeds of broccoli. They look a lot like alfalfa, and taste similar too. With between 10–100 times more sulforaphane than broccoli, these sweet little sprouts are bona fide longevity superstars.

You can buy broccoli sprouts already sprouted from some organic shops and local farmers markets, but sprouting them yourself is actually very easy and so much fun — and you can do it on your kitchen windowsill.

Blue-Green What?

Neurodegenerative diseases are one of the leading causes of premature death.[20] So it makes sense that if we can take steps to prevent these kinds of diseases (think: Alzheimer's disease, Parkinson's disease and Lewy body disease), we'll be doing good things for our life and health span. Luckily, there are plenty of simple steps you can take to give your neuronal system — and especially its engine, the brain — the best chance of reaching "old" age in tip-top shape.

Remember in Chapters 8 and 9, when we discussed the importance of movement and exercise on your brain? Here's your reminder: exercise is a potent preventer of neurodegenerative disease and brain aging.[21] So let's not forget the importance of those 10,000 steps!

There's another rock star for brain health that you may not be so familiar with, and it actually comes from (drum roll, please) sludge. Yes, sludge — specifically the blue-green type of algae most commonly consumed as spirulina. An important enzyme found in spirulina (superoxide dismutase — say that three times fast!) has been shown to reduce oxidative stress damage[22] and protect against Parkinson's disease.[23] It has also been shown to improve physical performance when taken before exercise as well as to increase fat loss during exercise.[24] And not to sing its praises too highly, but spirulina has also been shown to improve obesity markers[25] and reduction of plaque build-up in arteries.[26] Hands in the air if you want some of that!

You can buy spirulina in powder form and add it to your smoothies or sprinkle it on top of salads. It's also available pressed into tablets.

Nicotinamide Adenine Dinucleotide

Say what?! It has a long name but nicotinamide adenine dinucleotide — aka NAD^+ — is one of the coolest cats on the longevity biohacking and science scene.

Found in every cell in your body, NAD^+ is a critical coenzyme that's involved in hundreds of metabolic processes like cellular energy, skin health, and mitochondrial health. However, it declines as we age and this reduction has been implicated in the onset and progression of multiple age-related conditions such as neurodegenerative disease (there it is again!) and the hallmarks of aging, such as increased DNA damage and mitochondrial dysfunction, and decreased autophagy (aka cleanup of damaged cells).[27]

In a nutshell, more NAD$^+$ may equal more happy and healthy years. It can be synthesized in our body from various niacin precursors (vitamin B3) or niacin equivalents and the amino acid tryptophan, so boosting levels of NAD$^+$ by supplementing with these precursors has been shown in animal studies to improve health span and life span.

As with all breakthroughs in this field, the internet is rife with cheap NAD$^+$ boosters, so be sure to only take a clinically validated supplement. (You'll find an up-to-date list of our recommended suppliers on www.TimeMagic.me.).

Protect Your Pearly Whites

Poor oral health has been linked to increased risk of coronary heart disease, diabetes, pneumonia, and stroke.[28] A Harvard study even showed that the bacteria that causes gingivitis, *P. gingivalis,* produces toxins that accumulate in the brains of Alzheimer's patients.[29]

You may be thinking, "Well, I already brush my teeth every day, I'm covered!" But to that we'd say: not so fast, amigo. Brushing your teeth is a good start but there is a lot more you can do to ensure you not only keep your teeth, but reduce your risk of premature death from these very unnecessary modern lifestyle diseases.

Melissa grew up on a typical western diet and brushed her teeth diligently every day, yet as early as 21 years of age she was showing worrying signs of major gum loss and is still dealing with this issue today.

Nick, on the other hand, was fortunate that his dad was a dentist ahead of his time, and from the age of ten he had Nick using a Waterpik®, a water flosser. It still baffles us to this day how anyone can live without a Waterpik®, which is essentially a small device that sprays a powerful fine jet of water in between your teeth. You will never forget the squeaky clean feeling after your first Waterpik®. Given the huge and wide-ranging risks you leave yourself open to by *not* looking after your oral health, this inexpensive and easy-to-use gadget is a true no-brainer when it comes to Everyday Longevity.

If you are grabbing your phone and googling "Waterpik" right now (you superstar, you) then be sure to go for one of the more powerful models over the battery-operated model. Personally, we love the Traveler™ Water Flosser which is compact and more powerful than others on the market. It also means you won't run out of battery mid-pik, which is an annoying habit of the lesser models.

Another "Holy moly, how can you live without this?" strategy is tongue scraping. Apart from just feeling so damn amazing when you do it, science has shown that scraping your tongue can reduce total bacteria and plaque build-up.[30] Buy a tongue scraper for a couple of bucks at your local chemist or health food store, drag that bad boy over your tongue every morning on waking, and watch in amazement and/or horror at the shockingly huge amounts of bacteria you scrape off.

Speaking of bacteria, did you know that your toothbrush may actually be doing you harm? Yup. When was the last time you properly disinfected your toothbrush? This morning, right? Most likely not. Toothbrushes have been shown to house millions of bacteria, many of which cause gum disease. *Gross*. Fear not, an inexpensive spray of 1 percent hydrogen peroxide can suppress the growth of bacteria. There are now also many easy-to-use UV light sterilizers widely available for home use.

A final point about the bacteria in your mouth — this time, the good kind. There's a whole ecosystem of bacteria in your mouth, the same as in your gut. In fact, the two are directly correlated. So everything you do for your gut microbiome (like getting your 30 "plant points" each week, which we know you're doing, right?!) is also great for your oral microbiome.

THE TIME MAGIC ORAL ROUTINE

Here are our Time Magic recommendations for sparkly clean teeth, pink healthy gums, and breath so fresh you can pash upon waking (well, not quite — but close!).

Step 1: When you wake up, start by brushing your teeth with your sterilized toothbrush. Toothpastes bought in supermarkets are not your best bet as they generally contain many toxic chemicals. Instead, opt for making your own or buy a healthy toothpaste from an organic store.

Step 2: Sterilize your toothbrush.

Step 3: Scrape your tongue using a stainless steel or copper tongue scraper, available at most health food shops.

Step 4: Use your brand spanking new Waterpik (and thank us later!). We also recommend doing some regular flossing once a day or every couple of days as a different way to massage your gums and keep them squeaky clean.

Step 5: With a small amount of water in your mouth, add a drop or two of On Guard® essential oil and swish it around your mouth and gargle for 30 seconds to a minute. Rinse and repeat, literally. Do the same after breakfast so you can start your day feeling fresher than a sun-kissed daisy, and before bed to prevent pathogenic bacteria build up while you sleep.

Speaking of Sleep ...

While sleep has already had its own worthy deep-dive in Chapter 8, it's so crucial to your health and longevity that we just have to mention it again here.

We can't recommend highly enough to start optimizing your sleep by using the strategies outlined in Chapter 8. Whatever you may have going on in your life right now, whether it's stress, weight you can't seem to lose, insomnia, relationship issues, fatigue, or even chronic disease, all of these and more can benefit from not only increasing the amount you sleep, but also the quality of that sleep.

If we had to pick a couple of essential Time Magic Tricks to employ right now, they would be:

1. Get into bed early and be asleep no later than 10 p.m. Wake up no later than 6 a.m.
2. Have a light dinner (and not too much liquid) 2–3 hours before you get into bed.

Mobility Mojo

When you do make it to 70, 80, or 100 years of age, you want to be able to enjoy yourself, right? We certainly do — we want to be running around with our grandkids, dancing, doing yoga, surfing, lifting weights, and making love right until the end of our time on this planetary playground.

In order to do all those things, it's absolutely crucial to focus on your mobility — that is, how your body and joints move through a range of motion.

Nick's Nana Ruth could touch her toes well into her nineties, and if not for an unfortunate fall and broken hip, may have lived a decade more. Some reports show that up to 50 percent of patients with hip fractures die within six months and sadly many of those who do manage to beat the odds and survive never recover their baseline independence and function.[31]

Our ability to sit and get up off the floor has also been shown to be a predictor of how long we live, so start practicing this skill now.[32] Extra points if you can do the sit-to-stand test by getting up off the floor without your hands. Go on, give it a go. If you were surprised how hard this is to do, don't sweat it — just make a note to work on this each day until it becomes effortless.

Another skill to work on: walking up and down stairs. Even something as simple as this is a powerful predictor of how long you live and how you die.[33] Again, extra points if you are over 70 years of age and do not need to use the handrail.

Another act of mobility that's particularly worth focusing on is the squat. Yes, the simple act of being able to squat can be a predictor of not only your longevity,[34] but your freedom of movement in your later years. (In fact, one of the tests that scientists use to predict life span is called the squat test!)

You can make squatting an incidental part of your day simply by squatting on the toilet instead of sitting — yep, we want you to squat on the pot! The first time Melissa accidentally walked in on

Nick perched on the throne in a deep squat, wearing nothing but his birthday suit, was a moment to remember. Now, she doesn't even blink! It's not glamorous, but it works wonders — not only for your hip flexibility, but your bowel movements as well, by putting your body into a position that better facilitates the evacuation of your poop.

If the idea of perching on the porcelain is too much for you, then grab yourself a Squatty Potty®, which is a slightly more glamorous way to get your body into a more natural position for some glorious *smooth moves*.

Easy-Squeezy

Grip strength has also been shown to be an important biomarker for older adults.[35] This does not mean that if you rush out and buy a grip strength trainer, you are magically going to live longer. (We wish!) It's more of an indicator of your overall mobility, limb strength, bone density, muscle strength, and how you are aging in general.

By all means, though, grab yourself a grip strength meter, also known as a hand dynamometer, so you can assess your baseline strength. It doesn't matter so much what your strength rating is, more that it doesn't decline over time. In fact, ideally, you want to be increasing it over time, as this is an indicator that you're becoming stronger overall. And on that note, let's talk about the best way to build your overall strength.

Muscle Up

Have you heard of sarcopenia? It's the loss of skeletal muscle mass and strength as we age. It not only contributes to type 2 diabetes, frailty, physical disability, loss of independence, and poor quality of life, but has been shown to be a predictor of reduced longevity in older adults.[36]

For that reason building and maintaining muscle is high on the list of priorities when it comes to Everyday Longevity. It doesn't matter whether you prefer pumping weights at the gym, doing bodyweight exercises, using resistance bands, or some other activity; it only matters that you're doing something to build those muscles.

Three Nutritional Ninjas for Extra Muscle Mojo

1. PUMP UP THE PROTEIN

Consuming adequate protein is an important part of any muscle-building and fat-loss program. Our favorite source is legumes (beans and pulses), the protein powerhouses of the plant world!

2. GET YOUR VITAMIN C

Vitamin C, also known as ascorbic acid, is an essential nutrient, widely recognized for its antioxidant properties and abundantly found in many fruit and vegetables. By making sure you are consuming vitamin C-rich fruit and vegetables such as berries, lemons, limes, oranges, kiwifruit, capsicums (bell peppers), tomatoes and cruciferous vegetables, you are also reducing your chances of losing that precious skeletal muscle mass.[37]

3. THE OTHER C: CREATINE

While resistance training alone has been shown to improve musculoskeletal health during aging, the combination of creatine supplementation and exercise has been shown to lead to greater physiological and health benefits, specifically in the elderly, as it relates to skeletal mass and strength.[38] While we do synthesize creatine in our liver from our body's amino acids, it is still necessary to get a top-up from our diet. Fortunately, creatine is one of the most studied and safest supplements and one that can significantly move the needle when it comes to building and maintaining optimal skeletal muscle mass.

We recommend looking for a clinically tested brand (you'll find our favorites listed on www.TimeMagic.me) and supplementing a healthy diet with 3–5 grams per day.

The Time Magic Weekly Movement Routine

Now that we understand why muscle and mobility are so important for your quality and length of life, how do we go about putting together a consistent and simple routine that maximizes all the benefits of the various types of exercise available to us?

A recent study showed that people who ran six to eight kilometers per week (which, broken down into smaller daily pieces, would be around 15–20 minutes per day for most people), were 40 percent less likely to die from a heart attack and 45 percent less likely to die from all causes of mortality.[39]

In fact, even as little as just ten minutes a day of moderate exercise has been shown to add years to your life.[40] But this is Time Magic and you want to know what will move the needle the most in the least amount of time, right?

It makes sense that if we are strong (i.e., have good muscle mass), can move our body through all ranges of motion (i.e., have great mobility) and exercise regularly (i.e., have bangin' cardiovascular health), overall, we are going to be healthier. But to take it to the next level, we want to switch on our longevity genes and create more mitochondria (the microscopic battery power units of our cells), and to do this, we need to increase our breathing and heart rate.

Even though humans really were born to run, it's safe to say that running is something that not everyone loves to do. This is where HIIT comes in. High-intensity interval training (HIIT) is incredibly efficient at doing all of the above — especially at switching on those genes associated with youth[41] — and the good news is that it's fast and easy.

So let's pull together everything we've learned into a "choose your own adventure" Time Magic Workout Routine. There are multiple types of exercise we want to touch on to give ourselves the best chance at living a long and happy life. They are:

1. **Resistance training:** Dumbbells, barbells, resistance bands, kettlebells, medicine balls, sandbags, body-weight training, calisthenics.

2. **Low-intensity exercise:** Walking, light jogging, swimming slow laps, using an elliptical machine, cycling at a casual pace. (At this level of intensity, you should be able to carry on a conversation easily.)

3. **Moderate-intensity exercise:** 20–40 minutes of yoga, Pilates, playing a game of tennis, jogging, brisk walking, dancing, gardening, walking stairs, swimming laps, cycling. (Aim to be working hard enough that you're puffing but can still talk.)

4. **High-intensity exercise:** Calisthenics, rowing machine, bike machine, stair climber machine, kettlebells, rope jumping. (If you're puffing so hard it's a challenge to talk, you've nailed it!)

5. Mobility and stretching: Gentle yoga, foam rolling, stretching, mobility exercises, Pilates, squatting, getting up off the ground hands-free, ground-based movement.

How you mix and match these options is up to you, but you will want to design your routine to include all five categories to maximize your longevity benefits. Ideally, you want to hit all five categories (or as close as possible) most days, but at the very least a few times per week.

MELISSA: MY ROUTINE

Since becoming a mama, I now like to keep my training short and effective. Some mornings I will do a brisk 30–45-minute walk (medium-intensity) in nature. Other mornings I will do a 30–45-minute workout of weight training using kettlebell, dumbbells, Swiss ball, resistance bands, and TRX (resistance training) with a program from my trainer (I usually do this three times per week).

At lunchtime, Nick and I usually take our daughter to the beach, which involves walking up and down a big flight of stairs to the beach (carrying our daughter, which definitely ups the intensity!) and playing at the beach — running in and out of the water, kicking the ball, and lots of laughing (low-intensity).

On top of all this, throughout the day, we are getting up and down off the floor with Bambi, rolling around, having tickle fests and kitchen dance parties, which is all extra incidental exercise.

Each night, we wind down together at 7 p.m. when Bambi is asleep by going into our bedroom and doing mobility exercises and foam rolling (which is a great way to drop your nervous system into a parasympathetic state and feel extra relaxed before bed).

NICK: MY ROUTINE

We like to tag-team our exercise, and get a good chunk of it done before our daughter wakes up at 7 a.m. So while Melissa is out for her walk, I'm working on mobility and foam rolling between 5:30 a.m. and 6:30 a.m. after doing my 5 a.m. meditation.

I then go for a similar brisk walk along the ocean (medium-intensity) and sprint up every hill I come across (high-intensity). This is then followed by resistance band training (resistance) five times per week, with a focus on muscle hypertrophy for increased muscle mass.

As Melissa said, we go to the beach as a family around lunchtime (low-intensity) and spend the evenings foam rolling and doing more mobility.

On top of all that, I also surf (medium-intensity) and rock climb (medium-intensity) with Leo on the weekends.

I also leave my Inertia Wave® — a portable full-body resistance training kit that looks like battle ropes — set up on the balcony, so when I walk past I can squeeze in a quick mini-workout for metabolic conditioning.

When I'm working in my studio, I also set a timer to remind me to get up every 25 minutes and move my body. This is usually more foam rolling or mobility while doing singing practice to keep my vocal muscles in shape. (I don't love doing singing practice, but I don't mind Time Magic stacking this in between work moments.)

Neither example is very complicated. We've simply found a way to work each of the five categories into our days. We also work with our natural preferences, so that we actually enjoy our routines. For example, Nick doesn't love high-intensity training but enjoys doing some sprints while he is on his morning walk. Finding a routine you enjoy is crucial, otherwise you'll always battle with consistency.

To help get your creative juices cranking, we've included two sample workout routines for you below.

TIME MAGIC WEEKLY ROUTINE: BEGINNERS

This is great for anyone who is starting out on their fitness journey.

Resistance training: Two times per week, starting with body weight and light weights.

Low-intensity exercise: A daily easy walk for 30–60 minutes (aim for 10,000 steps per day).

Moderate-intensity exercise: Twice per week, try taking a Yin yoga class, beginner Pilates class, walk stairs, or any other type of exercise where you get your heart rate up.

High-intensity exercise: There are so many great free HIIT apps you can download or free workouts on YouTube. Aim for 4 minutes once a week. This can be broken into 60 seconds on, 30 seconds off (repeat four times), or any interval that feels good for you.

Mobility and stretching: Get comfortable with being on the floor and start working on your mobility. A quick search on YouTube will find many great daily mobility routines. Find one or a few that you like and commit to this daily. Without mobility, we don't have quality of life. Once you are done with that, grab your foam roller and roll your whole body. Vibrating rollers are really great at easing tension and amplifying your results. This is also a great time to practice getting up off the floor without using your hands, or if you are a bit older, just getting up and down off the floor as many times as you can is great.

TIME MAGIC WEEKLY ROUTINE: NEXT LEVEL

This routine is great for anyone who has graduated from the beginner level, or for those of you wanting to really maximize your longevity.

Resistance training: Three to five times per week

Low-intensity exercise: Daily easy walk for 60 minutes (aim for 10,000 steps per day)

Moderate-intensity exercise: Two to four times per week

High-intensity exercise: Two to three times per week

Mobility and stretching: Daily

If you are wondering where you will find the time to integrate the Time Magic Weekly Movement Routine into your life, well, you are a Time Magic magician now and there are many levers you can pull from this book to create the space needed to make your happiness and longevity a priority. Going to bed an hour earlier and waking up an hour earlier may be all it takes to radically transform your mindset, physique, and add healthy years to your life.

And when in doubt, or when you're feeling unmotivated, ask yourself: if not you, who? If not now, when?

Get Cold, *Very* Cold

Chronic inflammation is a key driver in the aging process and a contributing factor behind many debilitating conditions such as Alzheimer's disease, asthma, cancer, heart disease, rheumatoid arthritis, and type 2 diabetes.[42] By following the Time Magic lifestyle, you will already be negating many of the factors responsible for inflammation. But there is one superstar preventive activity that has been practiced for hundreds, if not thousands of years.

Cold exposure is basically the practice of exposing your body to very cold temperatures with modalities like cold water immersion, local cryotherapy, and whole-body cryotherapy. Some of the many benefits include an increase in new mitochondria,[43] weight loss and improved metabolic health,[44] improved immune function,[45] and a decrease in depression.[46]

The easiest way to get your cold fix is with an ice facial. Aside from being great for your skin and touted by celebrities as a secret for looking younger, the ice facial also stimulates your parasympathetic nervous system (which is great for stress relief). Here's how to do it.

TIME MAGIC TRICK: GIVE YOURSELF AN ICE FACIAL

The night before you want to do an ice facial, fill a large bowl about one-third full of filtered water and freeze overnight.

The next morning, before you shower, take the bowl out of the freezer and fill it with water to about 5–3 centimeters below the rim.

After your shower, give the water a quick stir to mix the cold water around. Have a towel in arm's reach, then it's go time: with your eyes and mouth closed, dip your face into the cold water. Keep it there for as long as is tolerable. You might only be able to last 10–20 seconds at first, but you'll soon build up your icy stamina!

You can also dip your toes in the cold-therapy world by experimenting with cold showers. Start by having a normal shower, then at the end, turn it to cold and stay under for at least 30 seconds. Build up your tolerance by extending the time under cold water until you can comfortably do it for several minutes. Alternating from hot for one minute to cold for one minute, back and forth, is a great way to increase circulation in your body. Just try it once and try not to feel totally alive by the end. It will get all your cells dancing!

The Magic Wand

What if we told you there was a magic wand you could wave that with a single flourish could:

+ Reduce your risk of dying from cardiovascular disease by 27 percent;
+ Reduce your risk of developing Alzheimer's disease by 65 percent;
+ Reduce your risk of dying of *any* premature causes by a whopping 40 percent?

Such a thing *does* exist. It's not a wand, of course. And it's not magic; it's science: the science of sauna. Yep, turns out getting hot and sweaty in a small space seemingly has magical health benefits.[47]

On top of all the above outcomes, regular use of a sauna has been shown to reduce levels of inflammation in the body,[48] reduce symptoms of depression,[49] reduce oxidative damage, increase growth hormone and muscle mass,[50] facilitate the excretion of certain toxicants like heavy metals[51] and BPA[52] that bioaccumulate in the body, and much more. Once again, this all adds up to more years in your life and more life in your years.

Many health clubs and gyms have a sauna you can use, so you may find your existing gym membership already covers the cost of using this incredibly powerful Everyday Longevity trick. Now that's some serious longevity leverage!

If you're after a home option and are tight on space, we had an infrared sauna device installed in our shower at our previous home and loved it.

Our final longevity tool is one that might surprise you more than any other.

Love Your Way to a Long, Healthy Life

We've touched on the Blue Zones already in this chapter — they're the areas around the globe that have a disproportionate number of centenarians and generally long-lived healthy people. These Blue Zones have been studied extensively, and one of the more surprising findings from these regions is that love and spirituality seem to have a big impact on longevity.

Research from the Blue Zones found that people who attend a faith-based service four times per month can expect to add 4–14 years onto their life expectancy. (Like we've said so many times in this chapter: that's huge!) And here's the kicker: it doesn't seem to matter what denomination you choose, it's merely the act of practicing your faith in a community that's enough.[53]

Dan Buettner, the founder of the Blue Zones project, suggested that believing in a religion might allow people to relinquish the stresses of their everyday life and hand them over to a higher power. Whatever the reason, if faith and religion are important to you, know that they're also great for your longevity, too.

Another powerful insight from the Blue Zones is the importance of family to longevity. Long-lived cultures all seem to place great emphasis on family, with aging parents and grandparents usually living close by or in the home — an arrangement which has been shown to have beneficial health outcomes not just for the oldies but for the kids too.[54] Successful centenarians also tend to prioritize commitment to a spouse or life partner, and invest in their children with time of love.

So the research is in: you can literally *love* your way to a long life.

We don't know about you, but that's our favorite longevity tool of all.

Notes

1   Jung S., et al., "Fruit and vegetable intake and risk of breast cancer by hormone receptor status," *Journal of the National Cancer Institute*, 2013, 105, 219–236; Lee, J.E., et al., "Intakes of fruits, vegetables, vitamins A, C, and E, and carotenoids and risk of renal cell cancer," *Cancer Epidemiology, Biomarkers & Prevention*, 15, 2006, 2445–2452

2   Guo, W., et al., "A nested case-control study of oesophageal and stomach cancers in the Linxian nutrition intervention trial," *International Journal of Epidemiology*, 23, 1994, 444–450; Jeurnink, S.M., et al., "Variety in vegetable and fruit consumption and the risk of gastric and esophageal cancer in the European Prospective Investigation into Cancer and Nutrition," *International Journal of Cancer*, 131, 2012, E963–973

3   Kushi, L.H., Meyer, K.A. and Jacobs, D.R., "Cereals, legumes, and chronic disease risk reduction: evidence from epidemiologic studies," *The American Journal of Clinical Nutrition*, 70, 1999, 451s–458s

4   Gaesser, G.A., "Carbohydrate quantity and quality in relation to body mass index," *Journal of the American Dietetic Association*, 107, 2007, 1768–1780; McKeown, N.M., et al., "Whole-grain intake is favorably associated with metabolic risk factors for type 2 diabetes and cardiovascular disease in the Framingham Offspring Study," *The American Journal of Clinical Nutrition*, 76, 2002, 390–398; Flight I. and Clifton P., "Cereal grains and legumes in the prevention of coronary heart disease and stroke: a review of the literature," *European Journal of Clinical Nutrition*, 60, 2006, 1145–1159; Randi G., et al., "Dietary patterns and the risk of colorectal cancer and adenomas," *Nutrition Reviews*, 68, 2010, 389–408; Huang, T., et al., "Consumption of whole grains and cereal fiber and total and cause-specific mortality: prospective analysis of 367, 442 individuals," *BMC Medicine*, 13, 2015, 59

5   Hu, F.B. and Stampfer, M.J., "Nut consumption and risk of coronary heart disease: a review of epidemiologic evidence," *Current Atherosclerosis Reports*, 1, 1999, 204–209

6   www.hindustantimes.com/fitness/hara-hachi-bu-the-reason-why-the-japanese-live-a-100-years-or-more/story-pQyKhSsL7eQaZXEFYDY2BJ.html

7   Browning, J.D., Baxter J., Satapati S. and S.C. Burgess, "The effect of short-term fasting on liver and skeletal muscle lipid, glucose, and energy metabolism in healthy women and men," *Journal of Lipid Research 53*, no. 3, December 2011; 577–86. doi.org/10.1194/jlr. p020867; Brandhorst S., Choi I.Y., Wei M., Cheng C.W., Sedrakyan S., Navarrete G., Dubeau L., et al., "A periodic diet that mimics fasting promotes multi-system regeneration, enhanced cognitive performance, and healthspan," *Cell Metabolism*, 22, July 2015, no. 1: 86–99. doi. org/10.1016/j.cmet.2015.05.012; Wong S., de Cabo R., Bernier M., Diaz-Ruiz A., Rhinesmith T., Moats J., Ehrlich M., Eshaghi F., Corrales-Diaz Pomatto L. and Bosompra O., "Metabolic Flexibility: Interplay of Diet Composition and Intermittent Fasting on Healthspan," *Current Developments in Nutrition* 3, Supplement 1, June 2019: doi.org/10.1093/cdn/nzz044.p08-053-19

8   Stekovic S., Hofer S.J., Tripolt N., Aon M.A., Royer P., Pein L., Stadler J.T. et al., "Alternate Day Fasting Improves Physiological and

Molecular Markers of Aging in Healthy, Non-obese Humans," *Cell Metabolism*, 30, no. 3, September 2019: 462–76.e6. doi.org/10.1016/j.cmet.2019.07.016

9 www.sciencedaily.com/releases/2021/07/210722113004.htm

10 Thiele C.J., Hudson M.D., Russell A.E. et al., "Microplastics in fish and fishmeal: an emerging environmental challenge?," *Scientific Reports* 11, 2045 (2021). doi.org/10.1038/s41598-021-81499-8

11 "Dietary intake and biomarkers of alpha linolenic acid and risk of all cause, cardiovascular, and cancer mortality: systematic review and dose-response meta-analysis of cohort studies," *BMJ* 2021; 375 doi: doi.org/10.1136/bmj.n2213 (Published 14 October 2021)

12 Yang Y., Zhao L.G., Wu Q.J., Ma X., Xiang Y.B., "Association between dietary fiber and lower risk of all-cause mortality: A Meta-Analysis of Cohort Studies," *American Journal of Epidemiology*, 2015; 181:83-91

13 McDonald D., Hyde E., Debelius J., Morton J., Gonzalez A., Ackermann G., et al., "American Gut: an Open Platform for Citizen Science Microbiome Research," eCollection. May 2018: 3(3):e00031-18

14 Vermorken A.J., Andrès E., Cui Y., "Bowel movement frequency, oxidative stress and disease prevention," *Molecular and Clinical Oncology*, 2016 Oct;5(4):339-342. doi: 10.3892/mco.2016.987. Epub 2016 Aug 10. PMID: 27703675; PMCID: PMC5038884

15 www.ucsfhealth.org/education/increasing-fiber-intake

16 Tuohy K.M., Gougoulias C., Shen Q., Walton G., Fava F., Ramnani P., "Studying the human gut microbiota in the trans-omics era – focus on metagenomics and metabonomics," *Current Pharmaceutical Design*, 2009; 15(13):1415-27. doi: 10.2174/138161209788168182. PMID: 19442166

17 pubmed.ncbi.nlm.nih.gov/3966422/

18 www.ncbi.nlm.nih.gov/pmc/articles/PMC6885086/

19 https://nutritionfacts.org/2016/02/09/how-to-cook-broccoli/; pubmed.ncbi.nlm.nih.gov/29806738/

20 Varela L., Garcia-Rendueles MER., "Oncogenic Pathways in Neurodegenerative Diseases," *International Journal of Molecular Sciences*, March 2022; 23(6):3223. doi: 10.3390/ijms23063223. PMID: 35328644; PMCID: PMC8952192

21 www.sciencedirect.com/science/article/abs/pii/S0025619611652191

22   pubmed.ncbi.nlm.nih.gov/21697639/

23   pubmed.ncbi.nlm.nih.gov/23028885/

24   pubmed.ncbi.nlm.nih.gov/20010119/

25   pubmed.ncbi.nlm.nih.gov/?term=spirulina+obesity

26   pubmed.ncbi.nlm.nih.gov/20354344/; pubmed.ncbi.nlm.nih.
     gov/23684441/

27   Fang, E.F., Lautrup S., Hou Y., Demarest T.G., Croteau D.L.,
     Mattson M.P., and Bohr V.A., "NAD+ in Aging: Molecular
     Mechanisms and Translational Implications," *Trends in Molecular
     Medicine*, 23, no. 10, October 2017: 899–916. doi.org/10.1016/j.
     molmed.2017.08.001

28   pubmed.ncbi.nlm.nih.gov/29461088/; www.ncbi.nlm.nih.gov/pmc/
     articles/PMC8361186/

29   sitn.hms.harvard.edu/flash/2019/oral-bacteria-may-responsible-
     alzheimers-disease/

30   bmcoralhealth.biomedcentral.com/articles/10.1186/1472-6831-14-4

31   pubmed.ncbi.nlm.nih.gov/26016287/

32   pubmed.ncbi.nlm.nih.gov/23242910/

33   www.escardio.org/The-ESC/Press-Office/Press-releases/
     Performance-on-exercise-test-predicts-risk-of-death-from-
     cardiovascular-disease-and-cancer

34   de Brito L.B.B., Ricardo D.R., de Araújo D.S.M.S., Ramos P.S.,
     Myers J.and de Araújo C.G.S. "Ability to sit and rise from the floor
     as a predictor of all-cause mortality," *European Journal of Preventive
     Cardiology*, 2014, 21(7):892–898. doi: 10.1177/2047487312471759

35   www.ncbi.nlm.nih.gov/pmc/articles/PMC6778477/

36   pubmed.ncbi.nlm.nih.gov/24561114/

37   academic.oup.com/jn/article/150/10/2789/5897318

38   Candow D.G., Forbes S.C., Chilibeck P.D., Cornish S.M., Antonio J.
     and Kreider R.B. "Effectiveness of creatine supplementation on aging
     muscle and bone: Focus on falls prevention and inflammation," *Journal
     of Clinical Medicine*, April 2019; 8(4):488. doi: 10.3390/jcm8040488.
     PMID: 30978926; PMCID: PMC6518405

39   D. Lee, R.R. Pate, C.J. Lavie, et al., "Leisure-Time Running
     Reduces All-Cause and Cardiovascular Mortality Risk," *Journal of the
     American College of Cardiology* 54, no. 5, August 2014: 472–81, www.
     onlinejacc.org/content/64/5/472

40   *Ibid.*

41 Robinson M.M., Dasari S., Konopka A.R. et al., "Enhanced protein translation underlies improved metabolic and physical adaptations to different exercise training modes in young and old humans," *Cell Metabolism* 25, no. 3, March 7, 2017: 581–92, www.cell.com/cell-metabolism/comments/S1550-4131(17)30099-2

42 www.thelancet.com/journals/ebiom/article/PIIS2352-3964(15)30081-5/fulltext

43 Chung N., Park J. and Lim K., "The effects of exercise and cold exposure on mitochondrial biogenesis in skeletal muscle and white adipose tissue," *Journal of Exercise Nutrition & Biochemistry* 21, no. 2, June 2017: 39–47. doi.org/10.20463/ jenb.2017.0020

44 Dulloo, A.G., "Translational issues in targeting brown adipose tissue thermogenesis for human obesity management," *Annals of the New York Academy of Sciences* 1302, no. 1, October 2013: 1–10. doi.org/10.1111/nyas.12304

45 Janský L., Pospíšilová D., Honzová S., Ulicný B., Šrámek P., Zeman V. and Kamínková J., "Immune system of cold-exposed and cold-adapted humans," *European Journal of Applied Physiology and Occupational Physiology* 72–72, no. 5–6, March 1996: 445–50. doi.org/10.1007/bf00242274

46 Shevchuk, N.A., "Adapted cold shower as a potential treatment for depression," *Medical Hypotheses* 70, no. 5, January 2008: 995– 1001. doi.org/10.1016/j.mehy.2007.04.052

47 Laukkanen T., Khan H., Zaccardi F. and Laukkanen J.A., "Association Between Sauna Bathing and Fatal Cardiovascular and All-Cause Mortality Events," *JAMA Internal Medicine* 175, no. 4, April 2015: 542. doi: 10.1001/jamainternmed.2014.8187

48 Laukkanen T. and Jari A., "Sauna bathing and systemic inflammation," *European Journal of Epidemiology* 33, no. 3, December 2017: 351–53. doi: 10.1007/s10654-017-0335-y

49 Janssen C.W., Lowry C.A., Mehl M.R., Allen J.J.B., Kelly K., Gartner D.E., Medrano A., et al., "Whole-body hyperthermia for the treatment of major depressive disorder," *JAMA Psychiatry* 73, no. 8, August 2016: 789. doi: 10.1001/jamapsychiatry.2016.1031

50 Selsby, J.T., S. Rother, S. Tsuda, O. Pracash, J. Quindry, and S.L. Dodd, "Intermittent hyperthermia enhances skeletal muscle regrowth and attenuates oxidative damage following reloading," *Journal of Applied Physiology*, 102, no. 4, April 2007: 1702–7. doi: 10.1152/

japplphysiol.00722.2006

51   Kuennen M., Gillum T., Dokladny K., Bedrick E., Schneider S. and Moseley P., "Thermotolerance and heat acclimation may share a common mechanism in humans," *American Journal of Physiology-Regulatory, Integrative and Comparative Physiology* 301, no. 2, August 2011: R524–R533. doi: 10.1152/ajpregu.00039.2011

52   Lang I.A., "Association of urinary bisphenol a concentration with medical disorders and laboratory abnormalities in adults," *JAMA*, 300, no. 11, September 2008: 1303. doi: 10.1001/jama.300.11.1303

53   Buettner D. and Skemp S., "Blue zones: Lessons from the world's longest lived," *American Journal of Lifestyle Medicine*, July 2016; 10(5):318-321. doi: 10.1177/1559827616637066. PMID: 30202288; PMCID: PMC6125071

54   *Ibid.*

CONCLUSION

Your Time Is Now

Clayton Christensen was one of the greatest business minds of our time. One of his theories — the theory of disruptive innovation — has been called "the most influential business idea of the early twenty-first century."[1] He was an icon who made a legendary impact. But his thoughts on that impact are not what you might expect.

After a diagnosis of cancer in 2010, Christensen wrote the following in an article for *Harvard Business Review*:[2]

> *I have a pretty clear idea of how my ideas have generated*
> *enormous revenue for companies that have used my research;*
> *I know I've had a substantial impact. But as I've confronted*
> *this disease, it's been interesting to see how unimportant that*
> *impact is to me now.*

Those words, when we read them, hit us hard — especially the last line. So did the title of the article itself: "How Will You Measure Your Life?"

It seems that Christensen's answer to that powerful question shifted after his life-threatening diagnosis. It's not a stretch to imagine that what he once perhaps *thought* would be important to him, turned out not to be.

So we want to ask that same powerful question of you, here, as we come to the end of this book: how will you measure your life?

Throughout these pages, we've talked a lot about the only objective, quantifiable metric that we humans have to measure life: time. Hours, days, weeks, months, and years. We've walked you through strategies — both modern and ancient, science-backed and esoteric — that can help you reclaim your time and make more of it. This is all incredibly valuable to know. It's all life-changing information.

But we all know deep down that mere length is not the goal. "How long" is not the metric that matters. After all, a serial killer can live to 100, while we're betting that you, like us, have known some — even many — beloved souls who've been taken too soon.

So how should we measure our lives? How will you measure yours?

For many of us, in the past, the answer to this question has tilted towards the professional or the financial: our life's worth wound up tightly in how much we earn, how much we get done, how much recognition we've received, and how many ripples we create through our external work and achievements.

We hope that in reading this book, you've embraced some different kinds of measures for yourself. Such as how **intentional** you are with your hours, how much **meaning** you infuse into your days, how much **joy** you share with your loved ones, how deeply you **honor** your own needs, how closely you align with your **values**, how **authentically** you share your gifts, and how much **purposefulness** you bring to your life as a whole.

These are not the topics of an ordinary time management book.

But as you know, Time Magic is not time management. And this is no ordinary book.

And still, despite all this, we want to talk to you one last time about length. Because here's the thing: your life here on this planet, no matter how long you live, is — in a universal sense — fleeting.

In the scheme of things — from the moment of the Big Bang; to the first signs of life, to the dinosaurs roaming the earth; to the Neanderthals painting on cave walls; to the *Homo sapiens* hunting and gathering; to the last woolly mammoths; to Cleopatra gazing over the pyramids; to Da Vinci painting his masterpieces; to the invention of the telegram; to the rise of the smartphone; to you sitting here reading this page — the portion of time that we get to play with on this planet is exceedingly, mind-blowingly, blink-and-you'll-miss-it short.

Some people find this cosmic truth daunting. We propose that it's actually profoundly inspiring.

After all, who can't find joy in winning the incredible universal lottery that allowed us to come to this planet in the first place? Who isn't struck by wonder at the realization that they're not just a random inkblot on the galactic copybook, but the result of a billion years of intelligent evolution?

Some scientists suggest that the odds of you being born are one in 400 trillion. But if you take into account the full and extremely unlikely chain of events that led to your birth — not just the odds of your mother meeting your father, and the right sperm meeting the right egg, but *all* the ancestors and eggs and sperm who *also* had to meet in order for you to be you — then the probability of you existing at all comes out to just one in $10^{2,685,000}$. That's a 10 followed by 2,685,000 zeroes.[3]

To put that into perspective, you have a one in 1,222,000 chance of being struck by lightning.

A one in 292.2 million chance of winning the lottery.[4]

And the number of atoms in the known universe is 10^{80}.

Yet your odds of being here are one in $10^{2,685,000}$.

That makes you spectacularly special. A most favored child of the universe. A miracle made of stardust who has been gifted so many extraordinary things, including the ability to love and connect; to learn and grow; and to have thoughts, dreams, ideas, values, and feelings. You've also been given the incredible, extraordinary, irreplicable gift of *time*.

Your job now is to take what you've learned in this book and use that time *well*, whatever that means for you. This might mean making some changes, getting a bit uncomfortable, daring to disappoint others, saying yes to things that scare you, making some hard decisions, falling down, getting back up again, taking action, sitting still, speaking up, paying attention, diving deeper, living with more intention than you ever have before, and sticking with it.

But we know you're up to the task.

And we know that the reward — a life well lived — is intensely, undeniably, miraculously worth it.

So we'll leave you with one final question: **if not now, when?**

Your time is now. You can do this. Let the magic begin …

Notes

1   Wolfe A., "Clayton Christensen Has a New Theory," *Wall Street Journal*, 30 September 2016, retrieved 24 November 2019
2   Christensen, C.M., "How Will You Measure Your Life?" *Harvard Business Review*, 88, nos. 7–8, July–August 2010: 46–51
3   www.huffpost.com/entry/probability-being-born_b_877853
4   www.investopedia.com/managing-wealth/worth-playing-lottery/

ACKNOWLEDGMENTS

It takes a village to write a book (especially with children) and we are so grateful for ours.

First up, Jess Larsen — our epic book word-wizard. Thank you for your magic as always. Working with you is effortless and a dream come true. Thank you for being our sounding board. Your advice, support, love, care, and devotion to *Time Magic* is so appreciated. We know working on *Time Magic* took up a lot of your pie, but just know we are so grateful.

Our amazing publisher Catherine Milne at HarperCollins Australia, who has believed in our work from day one. You are a dream to work with and we could not imagine being on this journey without you by our side. Huge thanks also to the team at HarperCollins Leadership for believing in our message.

Our literary agent, Bill Gladstone. Thank you for always having our backs. You are family to us.

To our children Bambi and Leo for inspiring us to reclaim our time so we can spend more magical moments with you both. Especially you, Leo, for your patience. Your love, humility, and intelligence inspires us every day.

To all our beautiful friends and parents for your love, support, and feedback on titles, covers, and content. Doing life with you is the best.

To all our mentors and teachers, many of whom have been featured in this book. Thank you for following your dreams and doing your soul's work.

MELISSA

Thank you to my beautiful coauthor, husband, and biggest inspiration of all, Nick Broadhurst. You inspire me every day. You make me want to be the best version of me. I loved working on this "baby" with you (the start of many, I hope). Thank you for being my rock and for being my dream partner in life. I adore you.

NICK

Melissa, what a journey it has been to get to this point together. Not just with this incredible book, but our beautiful life too. You inspire me with your prolific output and dedication to your work. I am so honored that it is you I get to do life with. Thank you for being my one and always inspiring me to be a little bit better than I was yesterday.